I'm on LinkedIn—Now What???

A Guide to Getting the Most OUT of LinkedIn

By Jason Alba

Foreword by Bob Burg
Author of *Endless Referrals* and
Coauthor of *The Go-Giver*

20660 Stevens Creek Blvd., Suite 210
Cupertino, CA 95014

Published by Happy About®, a THiNKaha® imprint
20660 Stevens Creek Blvd., Suite 210, Cupertino, CA 95014
http://happyabout.com

Fourth Edition: March 2014
Third Edition: March 2011
Second Edition: December 2008
First Edition: September 2007
Paperback ISBN: 978-1-60005-254-5 (1-60005-254-1)
eBook ISBN: 978-1-60005-255-2 (1-60005-255-X)
Place of Publication: Silicon Valley, California, USA
Paperback Library of Congress Number: 2014932648

Trademarks

Warning and Disclaimer

Praise For This Book!

"Jason Alba's I'm on LinkedIn—Now What??? *is a must read for all social-networking 'non-believers.' Not only is it a useful tool for those looking to further their existing knowledge on how to optimize the many benefits of being 'Linked In,' it also serves as a treasure map to those who have yet to discover LinkedIn's hidden benefits and potential."*
Michelle A. Riklan, Managing Director, Riklan Resources, http://www.riklanresources.com, **and SelfGrowth.com,** http://www.selfgrowth.com

"As a career services professional, I recommend that every job seeker or professional currently working have a LinkedIn profile. Jason Alba's book is the perfect guide to help understand the important components of LinkedIn and how having an effective profile can pave the way to job opportunities. He does a great job explaining in logical, clear terms what the advantages of this site are and how candidates can come across more competitively as subject matter experts in their fields."
Dawn Rasmussen, President, Pathfinder Writing and Career Services, http://www.pathfindercareers.com

"Jason Alba has created an easy-to-follow guide for people of all skill levels. Anyone who wants to get more out of LinkedIn will find this book an invaluable resource. Jason's practical tips make LinkedIn's professional networking tool a breeze to set up and to keep up in today's marketplace. I highly recommend this."
Denny Stockdale, Author, *Conversations from the Neighborhood Ice Cream Shop: 8 Keys to Rediscovering Lost Dreams and Finding your Life's Calling*; and President, Stockdale Resource Group, http://www.stockdaleresourcegroup.com

"LinkedIn is a very powerful tool, and Jason Alba does a tremendous job of helping a new user get the most out of it."
Carl Chapman, Founder, CEC Search, http://www.cecsearch.com

"As a new 'learner' of LinkedIn, I was overwhelmed with the dynamics of it: how it works, what to put into my bio, etc. After reading Jason Alba's book, I not only felt at least like a semi-expert, but I have referred every single client in the world to Jason's fine information. It's simply a must-read for getting started and recognizing the value of the site. Good work, Jason."

Valerie Sokolosky, President, Valerie & Company,
http://www.valerieandcompany.com

"For both novices and skilled users alike, Jason's book offers a rare perspective on the value of LinkedIn for career management, while using a conversational tone that puts his readers at ease. I continue to recommend I'm on LinkedIn—Now What??? to job seekers, not only because they need a way to drill beyond the surface of the site, but also due to the little-known (but powerful) techniques he shares for business search and self-promotion. Jason's explanations of the strategy and reasoning behind LinkedIn as a personal PR and career transition tool are worth the price of admission alone!"

Laura Smith-Proulx, Executive Resume Writer, Certified Career Management Coach & Owner, An Expert Resume,
http://www.anexpertresume.com/

"To avoid commoditization, B2B companies must constantly expand their offerings and innovate how they sell, market, serve, and partner; in short, how they do business. If adding yet another product feature is no longer enough to differentiate, read this book. Shirman provides a treasure trove of strategies for staying relevant and valuable."

Erik Frieberg, Chief Marketing Officer, 10gen

"Ask any ten LinkedIn users how to use LinkedIn and, I bet you, at least nine of them will tell you to speak to Jason Alba! In this third edition, Jason wastes absolutely no time with fluff—it's not his style, anyway—and delivers a power-packed book that will turn even the most confused, non-LinkedIn user into a guru. Want to learn the secret to building your profile? It's in here. Not sure how to use Groups? Look no further. Bottom line: in this book, both the newbie AND the expert LinkedIn user are well served!"

Laura M. Labovich, Chief Career and Networking Strategist, Aspire! Empower! Career Strategy Group, http://thecareerstrategygroup.com/

Dedication

To Kaisie, Samantha, William, Taylor, Kimberly, and Daniel.

I appreciate the love and support you've given me since this journey began, back in 2006.

Acknowledgments

Thank you to the LinkedIn team, who continues to change the product, making a new edition so necessary! I once sent someone at LinkedIn a previous manuscript, and got an email back saying they had major changes planned that users would see in the next few months. That kind of response can be quite frustrating, but I choose to look at it as my job security!

I have gotten considerable strength and encouragement from many friends and acquaintances I've met since I got laid off in January of 2006. To the thousands of people who have purchased this book in a previous edition, thank you. Your comments on my blog (http://www.imonlinkedinnowwhat.com), your emails, and the evangelizing of my book have encouraged me to keep this work current.

There are many career professionals who have been instrumental in giving me feedback, advice, and tips to help me polish my message and delivery, and to make sure that what I present is what their professional, executive, and corporate clientele needs.

My publisher deserves a big hat-tip, as he has encouraged me, challenged me, and believed in me since we first met in 2007. Thank you, Mitchell and Happy About, for the opportunity to change my life and career path by becoming one of your authors.

Finally, deep gratitude and respect goes to my family, immediate and extended. I have seen them support my entrepreneurial dream, probably wondering what exciting thing would come up next. Their support has allowed me to enjoy the road I'm on and touch many lives as we talk about better ways to network, nurture relationships, and have more security for our future.

Contents

Foreword   Foreword by Bob Burg. 1

Part I   **Getting Started** 5

Chapter 1   **Introduction** 7

Chapter 2   **What Is LinkedIn?** 11

Chapter 3   **Your Profile** 25

Chapter 4   **Account, Privacy, & Settings** 35

Chapter 5   **Connecting with Others** 41

Part II   **Making It Work for You** 49

Chapter 6   **Finding Contacts** 51

Chapter 7   **Understanding Degrees of Separation** 57

Chapter 8   **Recommendations** 61

Chapter 9   **Jobs** 67

Chapter 10   **Companies** 71

Chapter 11   **LinkedIn Groups** 75

Part III   **Wrapping It Up** 83

Chapter 12   **LinkedIn for Personal Branding** 85

Chapter 13   **Shady Practices** 89

Chapter 14   **On Netiquette** 93

Chapter 15 | Complementary Tools and Resources 97

Chapter 16 | Conclusion......................... 103

Appendix A | LinkedIn for Job Seekers 105

Appendix B | LinkedIn for Sales Professionals........ 109

Author | About the Author 111

Books | Other Happy About Books............... 113

Figures

Figure 1   **Recommend Contact. 62**

Figure 2   **Clarify Relationship. 62**

Figure 3   **Written Recommendation. 63**

Figure 4   **Display Recommendation. 63**

Figure 5   **Show/Hide Recommendation. 64**

Foreword by Bob Burg

Several years ago, I began receiving requests from friends inviting me to join a new online membership site called LinkedIn. Soon I was getting emails from people I barely knew, asking me to "join their LinkedIn network." Although I'd been using the Internet for networking and relationship building for some time, I really wasn't all that interested in LinkedIn. Still, not wanting to hurt these people's feelings, I accepted.

I went through the process of posting my profile, but didn't do much with the site. As time went on, more and more people sent me invites.

Every so often, I'd be asked for help connecting someone with someone else, who apparently knew someone who knew someone I knew. From time to time, people from specific groups who'd read my book, *Endless Referrals*[1] would notice I was a LinkedIn member and ask me to contribute an article for their newsletter. I guess you could say I'd become a part of the LinkedIn community. But I wasn't really utilizing LinkedIn in any active or significant way.

Why not? No perceived need, and no desire. (You might remember those two reasons from Sales Training 101 as the two most common reasons prospects say "no.") And why didn't I have any perceived need or desire? Because I had no idea what to do or how to make LinkedIn a positive experience for me.

That's exactly where this book comes into play.

---

1. Bob Burg, Endless Referrals, McGraw Hill, 2005

Jason Alba has done a first-rate job of solving that challenge for me, and he will for you, too.

A former unemployed IT professional and business strategist, Jason found that finding a good job, even in a "job seeker's market," was a pretty daunting task. Today, he runs JibberJobber.com, a CRM website that helps job seekers organize their job search. In *I'm on LinkedIn—Now What???*, he presents us with an actual system to tap into the power of the LinkedIn service.

And that's the key word here: system. That's what I was lacking in my early LinkedIn experiences.

Why is having a system so important? I define a system as "the process of predictably achieving a goal based on a logical and specific set of how-to principles." In other words, if it's been proven that by doing A, you'll achieve B, then you know that all you need to do is follow A and you'll eventually achieve B. As Michael Gerber points out in his classic, *The E-Myth Revisited*[2] (slightly paraphrased): systems permit ordinary people to achieve extraordinary results—predictably.

Whatever the B is you want to achieve here, *I'm on LinkedIn—Now What???* provides you with the A for getting it. After an excellent introduction explaining exactly what LinkedIn is and how it (basically) works, Jason then walks you through a guided tour of clear principles and powerful strategies for getting the most out of your LinkedIn experience.

While Jason sees LinkedIn as an excellent business-building tool, he also looks at the site with

---

2. Michael Gerber, *The E-Myth Revisited*, HarperCollins, 1995

a carefully critical eye. Jason himself began achieving great success utilizing LinkedIn only after floundering with it his first few months, and he does not hold back in pointing out its weaknesses and suggesting areas where LinkedIn could improve and make its service more valuable for its members. I found especially re-freshing those passages where he points out the areas of LinkedIn where he has still not grasped its highest use. Someone that humble, I tend to trust.

Jason tells us that LinkedIn is not a replacement for your networking efforts (online or offline); rather, it is an excellent tool for facilitating some facets of your networking strategy. I absolutely concur. The creed of my Endless Referrals System®[3] is that "all things being equal, people will do business with, and refer business to, those people they know, like, and trust." And no computer or online medium is going to replace that personal connection—but it certainly can enhance it and provide potential networking contacts with more opportunities to connect. In this book, you'll learn how to do exactly that, whether it's for direct business, resources you need, helpful information, finding joint venture partners, hiring a new employee, or getting hired for a new job.

Something I particularly appreciate about Jason's approach is that he shows us not only how we can gain value from LinkedIn, but, just as important, how we can utilize LinkedIn to provide value to others. As any true networker knows, this is not only immensely satisfying in its own right, but it is also the best way to receive even more value oneself.

As you travel through this excellent guide, be prepared to learn from a man who has done his homework. Jason has learned what he knows the hard way, through trial and error, both his own and

---

3. http://www.burg.com

many other people's, and put it all between the covers of a book so that you and I can learn it all the easy way!

Best wishes for great success.

Bob Burg
Author of *Endless Referrals* and Coauthor of *The Go-Giver*
http://www.burg.com

Part I
Getting Started

Part I is all about getting started on LinkedIn.

- Chapter 1 talks about my personal experience with getting started, and why I decided to write this book.

- Chapter 2 talks about what LinkedIn is and isn't, helping you understand its capabilities and limitations.

- Chapter 3 is a crash course on your profile, and what you can do to set it up to increase your chances of being found by others and leave a favorable impression on those who find your profile.

- Chapter 4 talks about setting up your Privacy & Settings so your interaction with the website reflects your needs (and so you don't feel like you are getting spammed from LinkedIn).

1 Introduction

When I revised the first edition of this book, back in 2008, I was embarrassed to find over five hundred changes that I needed to make. I was shocked to find more than a dozen changes, much less hundreds and hundreds! I spent a lot of time researching and writing, editing and revising, and by the time the last draft went to the publisher I was sure it was as close to perfect as it could be. But when I sat down to update the book for the second edition, it seemed as if my highlighter deceived me. I actually agreed with the people who gave me poor reviews on Amazon. I almost went to Amazon myself just to give my own book a one-star review!

This is the fourth revision. The other editions of this book were based on changes in the technology. That is, changes that LinkedIn made, adding new features here, taking old features away, and adjusting the layout. I have not been alone in my frustration as LinkedIn makes changes. I've found LinkedIn advocates and evangelists who get weary of feeling like they aren't listened to, and they continually question why changes are made. I've even seen a fair amount of people who were once evangelists simply lose their enthusiasm for LinkedIn.

I feel like this revision is not based on LinkedIn's changes in technology and features. Of course, I'll update you on what you should know based on the new features, and removal of once-favorite features, but I have trained tens of thousands of people on using LinkedIn. I've heard a lot of questions and seen a lot of different uses and approaches. I've worked with college students from community colleges to the most elite schools, and trained and talked with people from many industries and professions. I've found there isn't necessarily a "best" answer for many strategies, and have grown to respect where you are, who your audience is, and what your objectives are. There are a lot of similarities in what we do and want to achieve with LinkedIn, and there are a lot of "yeah but" exceptions that I've seen. Some of the advice I'll share in this book might not apply to you directly, but it might make sense to think about something that doesn't exactly fit your strategy and see if you can creatively adjust it so you bring something new and fresh, and perhaps something novel that your audience hasn't seen before.

Over the years, social networking, social marketing, and corporate and personal branding have evolved. The tools we use to network and market and brand have also evolved. Online tools have come and gone. It's headspinning to try and keep up with the changes, especially with online tools. I don't have time to focus on whimsical fads, I'm interested in finding the best and the right tools, and learning how to exploit them to help me achieve a greater objective. I'm not an early adopter, but I do appreciate an effective tool and learning to use it the right way. If you want to learn how to make LinkedIn an effective tool for you, join me on this journey, in this book and on my LinkedIn blog.

Even as the tools have evolved, my own understanding of networking, relationships, marketing, and branding have evolved over time. I went from a job seeker who no one would talk to, to a new startup-CEO, to an author, to a speaker, to a seasoned startup-CEO. My goals and my relationships are different. My strategies and tactics are more refined. I follow up better and I am more strategic with my time. I also have an acute awareness of how overloaded professionals are.

If I had the time and resources, I might do a new edition of this book at least every six months. I can't do that, but I have something better for you. I blog regularly, sharing personal epiphanies, stories from others, and changes to my thinking based on what I continue to learn. If you are interested in personal career management, whether you are in a job search or you are preparing for a job search, check out the JibberJobber blog, which I update almost every day: http://www.jibberjobber.com/blog. If you are interested in LinkedIn strategies, whether for your personal career or for the company that employs you, check out my LinkedIn blog: http://imonlinkedinnowwhat.com.

I was first introduced to LinkedIn in February 2006 when I was walking out of a job seekers network meeting with a guy who came to tell us he had just landed a new job and wouldn't be coming back to our weekly meetings. I had connected with him because his resume looked almost

2 What Is LinkedIn?

Over the years, I've known people who thought LinkedIn was something that it really wasn't. It's critical to understand the boundaries of LinkedIn: what LinkedIn is and what it isn't. Depending on who you are and what you need, it may be extremely valuable, moderately valuable, or only slightly valuable. You might spend a lot of time on LinkedIn, with a proactive strategy, or you might spend hardly any time on LinkedIn, with a just-be-there, reactive, strategy.

So just what is LinkedIn? Some call LinkedIn a social network, others call it a business network (explicitly stating that it is not a social network), and others call it their contact management system. I agree that LinkedIn has elements of each of these tools, but I don't call it any of these things.

TIP: LinkedIn is a **tool**. Understanding the value proposition of LinkedIn, and its secondary benefits, should help you get the most out of your time or money investment in this tool.

LinkedIn is a tool to help you find others. You might connect with the people you find so they can add value to you, or so you can add value to them. Sometimes the value you see, or the value you can give, is not immediate. Sometimes the connection is the first step, and as your relationship strengthens and trust builds, the value you can give to one another increases. I've found this happens when I go beyond a surface, superficial relationship to a deeper relationship.

LinkedIn has a version of "degrees of separation," or connection. When you look at a person's profile it will show you how you are connected to them. Typically, you will see they are a first, second, or third degree contact, or that you are not any of those, but you are in the same Group. Here are some simple definitions of the three degrees of connection:

First-degree contact: someone who has agreed to connect with you, or who has sent you an invitation to connect, and you've accepted the invitation.

Second-degree contact: someone who is a first-degree contact of your first-degree contact. If you connect with me, all of your first-degree contacts become my second-degree contacts, and all of my first-degree contacts become your second-degree contacts.

Third-degree contact: first-degree contacts of your second-degree contacts. If you have millions of people in your network, they are usually going to be third-degree contacts.

Generally, it makes sense to connect with other people. Later in the book, we'll explore the idea of who to connect with, which has become quite a controversial topic. For now, let's leave it at this: LinkedIn is a tool to help you expand your network, both wider (with more first-degree contacts) and deeper (with the contacts of your first-degree contacts).

In addition to using LinkedIn to find people, LinkedIn is a place to be found. You should set up and optimize your own profile so others can find you. Your profile will probably have similarities to your resume (but it should not look like your resume). For example, you can list where you went to school, where you worked, dates of employment, what your tasks/roles were, and what your interests are. You can state what your current interests are, and you can choose what information to make visible to others, although I would not assume any expectation of privacy, no matter what your settings say. We'll talk about this in the "Your Profile" chapter.

The value of LinkedIn has grown as more people have joined. Imagine there were only one thousand people in LinkedIn, and they all lived in one city and belonged to one profession. Would LinkedIn be valuable to you? Not unless you happened to live in that city, or had an interest in that profession. Fortunately, there are over two hundred sixty million people who have created accounts on LinkedIn, which means you have a huge database of prospective contacts. And the value doesn't stop at finding new contacts.

Because of the huge number of members, and their respective diverse backgrounds and interests, LinkedIn has become a place where an immense amount of information gets shared. One of the strong commonalities between LinkedIn members is a desire to network either for business or professional reasons. LinkedIn is not really the site for music bands to advertise (like MySpace has been), although musicians do have profiles and can certainly use techniques from this book to promote their business. LinkedIn is not a site to look for dating opportunities, although I'm sure people have hooked up and perhaps even married as a result of relationships initiated on LinkedIn.

I find LinkedIn users to be a great source of knowledge about business and political issues, strategies and tactics, career management, job search ideas and job leads, consulting opportunities, and more. Because it is a place to share, ask, and recommend, LinkedIn can provide considerable value beyond just connecting with people.

What LinkedIn Is Not

Historically, LinkedIn has not been the social network with fun communities, video and joke sharing, and other such features. Facebook has those elements, as do sites like Tumblr, Twitter, Instagram, and other sites that seem to come and go. But LinkedIn has been adding a number of social features that brings it much closer to a Facebook or Twitter-like network. This isn't necessarily a good thing, and I've gotten many complaints that LinkedIn is trying to be something that has worked well for other sites, while losing the focus of adding value to people networking on LinkedIn.

On LinkedIn, you connect with others (who become your first-degree connections), see your connections' contacts (your second- or third-degree contacts), and possibly interact with them through various channels. In a previous edition of this book I wrote:

> With regard to social networking features, LinkedIn is not as feature-rich as the other sites, as it doesn't allow users to share blog posts, or leave messages and comments on your contacts' profiles in a conversational way for others to see.

This is no longer true. LinkedIn has added features that allow you to share blog posts, leave messages and comments on a contacts profile, and have conversations for others to see. LinkedIn is a bit more like Facebook in this regard, even while Facebook seems to have added features to become more like Twitter! With the ability to write a status update on your profile that your network can see and comment on, and have conversations (aka discussions) in LinkedIn Groups, LinkedIn is definitely more social than it ever was.

Let's switch gears from social to private relationship management. This is typically referred to as customer relationship management, which most people associate with a tool like Salesforce or ACT!. I have strong opinions about LinkedIn's new contact manager, mostly because of their policies, but also their history of discontinuing features.

In late 2011, LinkedIn acquired a CRM startup, and has added CRM features into the user experience. Aside from the CRM features not being as robust as CRM users need, the biggest issue I have is that LinkedIn has various policies that can get a user account shut down or otherwise penalized. I could handle being locked out of LinkedIn for a while because I can still go to Facebook, Google, and other tools to find information and do research. But I can't be locked out of my CRM for very long. Sooner rather than later, I'll need access to information that I've collected over the years, whether that is a special phone number or email address, or notes from a previous phone call. There is no other place I would have much of that information. If LinkedIn applies the same policies for their social environment (which addresses things like bullying, falsification, etc.), and a user gets locked out of their private database, it could mean lost work or opportunities.

Additionally, watching the pattern of discontinued features, I'm disheartened at the features LinkedIn promotes, but then eventually takes away. Even features that users love and rely on, like LinkedIn Answers, are subject to some executive's decision to take it away. While many people loved Answers, and some even petitioned to get it back, LinkedIn discontinued it, along with hundreds of thousands of great conversations (questions and answers) that are no longer accessible. Imagine if they decided to get rid of the CRM functionality, with private notes and information you have collected over time disappearing. Of course, that wouldn't happen, right? I'm not ready to completely trust LinkedIn with that information, so I'll take it elsewhere.

What kind of information am I talking about? In a previous edition of this book, I said:

A contact manager allows me to put contact information in a system and manage data for each contact. For example, I would put the name of a network contact and then update phone numbers, special dates (birthdays, graduations, etc.), spouse's name, and kids' names and ages.

The beauty of LinkedIn is that the person you are connected with can put in some of that information, and keep it current. However, what if someone goes in and wipes out their contact information, or if they don't keep their title current (because they aren't really using LinkedIn)? The burden of keeping the data updated is on them, but they might not care about how current it is. This means you might have better data than they have on their profile, so you really still need to keep their data updated. You can go into a contact's profile and add all kinds of information, including phone numbers, tags, notes, and more. The question is, should you?

I can't recommend LinkedIn as a relationship management tool. Don't get me wrong: LinkedIn is a powerful relationship tool, but it's not a relationship management tool I can confidently recommend. I would recommend using a CRM in conjunction with LinkedIn.

If you choose to use LinkedIn as a relationship management tool, make sure you **back up your contacts regularly**. On my JibberJobber blog, I wrote[5] about a career coach who mistakenly had her account disabled, wondering if she would ever get her network back. The account was eventually reinstated, but I imagine she has regularly backed up her contacts since then. Unfortunately, as of now, a backup does not export more than a few fields, which means any of the extra data you add will not be exported.

Clearly, LinkedIn is a networking tool. It is not, however, a networking **silver bullet**. Timeless networking principles such as "givers gain," etiquette, long-term relationship nurturing, and investing time and effort into relationships are critical. LinkedIn is not a *replacement* for your networking efforts (online or offline). It should be considered an excellent tool to complement your networking strategy.

Finally, LinkedIn is not a time hog. Once you get certain things set up (mostly your profile, group memberships, and preferences) you don't have to worry about spending much time in LinkedIn. Of course, if you have the time, you might derive value by incorporating some of the more advanced features we talk about in this book. The most

---

5. http://jibberjobber.com/blog/2008/07/17/linkedin-maintenance-do-this-right-now-or-else

common way I've seen people waste time on LinkedIn is by reading a lot of the articles and posts from others, but not doing any networking. If you treat LinkedIn as your source of information, as opposed to a networking tool, you'll probably not achieve the objectives you hoped to achieve (unless it was to learn about current events, which you can find in plenty of other sources).

Why Do People Use LinkedIn?

With over two hundred sixty million members in LinkedIn (there were about thirteen million members when the first edition of this book was printed, about twenty-eight million members when the second edition went to print, and about eighty million members when the third edition was written!), you are sure to find people who incorporate different strategies and techniques and have different motives for using LinkedIn. While it might boil down to "people meeting people," here are some examples of why people sign up for, or use, LinkedIn:

- **Professionals**—to develop their personal brand; to search for potential clients; to determine job titles and positions of prospects; to research potential contacts, companies, and industries.

- **Job seekers**—to get new network contacts; to find new leads and opportunities; to network into a company (do a search on a company and see who in their network might have an "in" where they want to interview); to establish a presence and hopefully be found by recruiters, hiring managers, and HR.

- **Recruiters and hiring managers**—to find prospects for open positions; to develop a rich network of prospective candidates; to search through connections of their connections, digging deeper into second- and third-degree contacts.

- **Entrepreneurs**—to develop an online presence; to establish a strong brand; to meet other entrepreneurs or potential business partners, customers, and investors; to build a team of cofounders and employees; to do market research; to get publicity.

There's a nice list at Web Worker Daily[6] that lists "20 Ways to Use LinkedIn Productively." I'm not going to pretend to know what you want to do on LinkedIn, but I encourage you to think about your goals and

---

6. http://gigaom.com/collaboration/20-ways-to-use-linkedin-productively

objectives. Turn your own goals and objectives into a list, and use it as you figure out where to spend time on LinkedIn, and how much time and effort you want to put into it.

Some of the tactics presented in this book may be appropriate for you, while other tactics may trigger ideas on how to get more out of LinkedIn. Remember, while LinkedIn may be useful to help you find and make connections, there are probably others who are looking for you. Be sure to have your profile updated and communicating the right things to people who are looking for you or your services. In other words, just because you are using LinkedIn to find others, don't forget that others might be evaluating you as a service provider, new talent, or for some other type of relationship.

LinkedIn Benefits

"I'm on LinkedIn—Now What???" That's the question I have heard since 2006! Once you sign up for an account, it isn't obvious where all the value comes from, even though LinkedIn has many evangelists. A common complaint I hear is based on the idea that people think they are signing up for this premier professional networking site and find their experience does not match up with all the hype. I think this is an issue of education and training, rather than technology. That's what this book is all about.

I have strong feelings about social networking. I personally feel "social-networked out." I regularly receive email invitations to social networks and wonder why I'm being invited. Sometimes the social networks are geography-based, sometimes they are interest-based. Usually the invitations don't appeal to me because I don't live in that particular geographic area, or I don't have much passion for that particular interest! Many invitations come without the inviter knowing he sent the invitation at all. For example, someone joins a new network just to see what it is all about and sometime during the sign-up process he grants access to his address book, which that network then uses to send invitations to all of his contacts on his behalf. Some people call this spam. Unfortunately, the person who granted access to his address book might not even realize all of his contacts were sent these emails! I have recently gotten invitations to connect with people on LinkedIn apologizing for the invitation. Be careful when you put your email or contact list username and password into any system.

Putting aside the general nuisances of social networking (some are more annoying than others), I've found it's definitely worth my time to participate actively in LinkedIn. I think about how my job search in 2006 would have been different had I been able to develop a LinkedIn network the size I have now (over seventy five hundred connections), and how my career management and even job performance, could have been better if I had a real LinkedIn strategy. Here are some of the benefits I have seen from my active participation in LinkedIn:

1. **Ability to be known.** Using LinkedIn, sharing my knowledge about LinkedIn on various Yahoo! and Google groups, commenting on LinkedIn blogs, and participating in LinkedIn Answers has made me much more visible to an audience that I'm interested in. When I talk about "personal branding," I am talking about being branded as a subject-matter expert and/or a thought leader. The ways I participate online help define my personal brand. I contribute, give, and share in a positive way to develop a good reputation in various online communities.

2. **Ability to be found.** I have strategically developed my LinkedIn profile to increase the chances of showing up in search results. What search results? I've put in key phrases so people who want to hire me can find me. Who is looking to "hire" you? If someone is looking for a project manager in Seattle, will they find you? If someone is looking for you, not by name but by profession, skills, attributes, location, will they find you? There are plenty of people looking for relationships that make sense for them, and they are using LinkedIn to find those people. Update your profile so when people look for you, they can find you!

3. **Ability to find others.** If you have a network that is "big enough," which LinkedIn indicates is around sixty-five contacts, you should have good enough reach when you do searches. I'm amazed when I do searches, and come up with certain results. For example, finding someone with the last name of "Jason" who has "Oracle" in their profile. I was only able to find this person through LinkedIn because I have a network that is "big enough." If I only had five first-degree contacts, I would not have found Mr. Jason who has Oracle in his profile. I have also found new, relevant contacts through my interactions on LinkedIn Groups.

4. **Opportunity to learn and share.** LinkedIn Groups is one of the most valuable tools in LinkedIn. I'm guessing Groups is the only reason some users log into LinkedIn! Some people have found new business, while others have received expert advice and information faster than any other option available to them. I have used Groups to share my personal and corporate brand, share news about products, and ask for input on a new project I'm working on), etc.

5. **Ability to connect with group members.** There are many closed or exclusive groups that you will have a hard time joining (such as alumni groups from colleges and universities). As of right now, there are almost two million groups on LinkedIn. When you join a group, you get access to the other group members. Group memberships can help you get in touch with people who share certain commonalities, such as geographic locations, associations, university affiliations, and professional or industry interests. I have joined dozens of groups that allow me to immediately message any other group member. I've strategically joined groups with members I want to develop relationships with just to make that initial contact, and then leave the group.

6. **Opportunity to show you are plugged in to current technology.** Having a LinkedIn account doesn't necessarily brand you as someone smart or technologically hip—but it can help! If you understand LinkedIn (and other tools) to some degree, you can communicate with others about these modern tools and resources. Of course, LinkedIn won't make you smarter than you already are, but being able to talk about online professional networking intelligently, and show that you have more than six connections, will likely indicate that you are serious and competent about networking, new technology, and your career. In today's world, it's practically expected to be up to speed on things like LinkedIn.

LinkedIn Limitations

The biggest problem people usually have with LinkedIn is not the technology (you can learn how to use technology from a book like this, Google searches, my blog, their blog, asking others, etc.), but the expectation that it will do amazing things for them, usually with minimal effort. By now, pretty much everyone has heard about LinkedIn. They know it is highly recommended because everywhere you go, you read or hear about it. Because of all of this, expectations are high, maybe to the point of unreasonable. It's as if you've heard of the greatest saw in the world, a saw that can create the most amazing things. You buy one, but it sits on the workbench. After weeks and weeks, it hasn't created anything. Do you blame the saw, or does the responsibility lie with you? It really is unreasonable to blame the tool if you, the creator, don't do anything with it.

You can't get on LinkedIn, and wait for value to come. Of course, you have to get on LinkedIn. If you want value, you should have an optimized profile, and then do some real work. To understand the kind of work you need to do, let's first understand what LinkedIn is NOT, so you can manage your expectations.

1. **LinkedIn is not your complete social environment.** LinkedIn has taken a while to offer social tools that we have seen in other sites, from the pioneering that MySpace had done to what we've come to expect with Facebook and other popular tools. For the most part, the slow evolution was just fine for many users, who didn't want the social functionality to clutter up their user experience, especially because they didn't go there for social interaction (like sharing funny YouTube videos). Instead, people went there to find talent and professional relationships. They went there to be found, and hopefully start meaningful relationships for their career or business. While MySpace and Facebook got clogged up with a bunch of distracting junk, LinkedIn remained clean, professional, and noise-free. In the last few years, we have seen many new social features in LinkedIn, including major enhancements to the status update (which makes it feel more like Twitter), group discussions (which became more important and powerful when LinkedIn removed Answers), and the companies pages (allowing Companies to have their own social conversations on their own page within LinkedIn). These types of changes bring us closer to more traditional social sharing, following, commenting, and community. The question is, with regard to social features, how much is enough, and how much is too much? Do we want LinkedIn to be all-things-social, or do we want it to be the best place to find and be found for our professional needs?

2. **LinkedIn does not represent your entire network.** Your entire network CANNOT be on LinkedIn. Are your plumber and your mechanic connected to you on LinkedIn? Mine aren't. Is everyone in your family on LinkedIn, and connected to you? I can't imagine anyone who has their entire family connected with them. Don't get hung up on the idea that your entire network is what you see on LinkedIn. Whether you have fifty first-degree contacts, or five thousand first-degree contacts, what you see on LinkedIn is only a subset of your entire network.

3. **LinkedIn does not give you complete control over the relationships you have.** You can only connect with me on LinkedIn if you are on LinkedIn, and you agree to be connected. What if you are not on LinkedIn? We'll never connect (unless I convince you to get on LinkedIn, but I rarely take the time trying to convince people to get a LinkedIn account). You simply cannot have every single person you know in real life connect with you as a first-degree contact. Furthermore, if I want to disconnect from you, I can do it with just a few clicks. You don't have any control over whether I stay in your LinkedIn network or not. That's why I strongly encourage you to use a complementary relationship management tool, since you can put whomever you want into that database, they won't know they are there, and they can't remove their record.

4. **LinkedIn does not allow you to control or change all of the information you want to track on your contact records.** As I mentioned earlier, people confuse LinkedIn with a relationship management tool, like a CRM that a salesperson would use to keep track of clients, prospects, and other contacts. Some of the most common CRM tools include Salesforce.com, GoldMine®, and ACT! There are hundreds of CRM tools available. My software, JibberJobber.com, was designed as a CRM for professionals in transition, and has been adopted by a number of contractors and freelancers as their CRM.

5. **LinkedIn can't really provide much privacy.** Information from your Public Profile will be available for people to see, no matter what you declare as "public" information. Your network will be available for others to see, even if you have the setting that says only you can see your connections. Not only can I see things you might have thought were private, I can grab a screenshot and share it anywhere online. These are big issues, and you should have no expectation of privacy anywhere online. Imagine sharing something privately, whether it is sensitive information your company might not want others to know, or news that you are in a job search (and your boss doesn't know yet), and your message getting out to the masses. It could be devastating. Here's something I learned from an information security professional: If you are looking for privacy, stay away from the Internet—period!

6. **LinkedIn has a closed communication system.** I don't like it when a service requires me to log into its website in order to get information or communicate with someone who is reaching out to me. I would like to reply to LinkedIn InMail messages from my email, but many times I need to reply from within the LinkedIn messaging system. I feel like this disrespects my time, probably just to have me go back into LinkedIn (so they can show they continue to get repeat visitors). It could be worse, though. At least the message from LinkedIn that I get in my email shows me the entire message so I don't need to login just to see what the message contains. I still wish I could quickly and easily reply from my email client, and regularly ask people to switch out of LinkedIn's mailing system to regular email.

There are other limitations. For example, some users say they are upset at the limit on the number of first-degree contacts you can have, which is thirty thousand. I seriously doubt this limit affects more than a handful of people. Even though there are limitations, I don't think LinkedIn should fix them all. It's like asking a saw to also be a hammer and a screwdriver. I am not alone in thinking that LinkedIn should not resolve all of these things! While it would be cool to have a super-system, a silver-bullet to solve all of my networking needs, I do not advocate LinkedIn as the total solution. Here's why:

First, LinkedIn still needs to polish and fine-tune its core functionality. As a software developer, I understand the danger of creating more features while the core is either incomplete or not architected to work with so many peripheral features. You may have used software that introduces cool bells and whistles that aren't relevant to you, while you still have complaints about the core functionality. It's always tempting to develop a broader offering, but it's usually not good for the end-users unless your core is really strong.

Second, in addition to spreading itself too thin with technical requirements, it can be an enormous distraction to design, support, and maintain non-core features. Designers need to make sure they do not break anything that exists (or should exist) in the core. The support team needs to learn new tools, philosophies, and rules. Introducing any new feature outside of the core can add exponential complexity with regard to maintaining the software and even the hardware. I'm not saying LinkedIn can't tackle any non-core features, but there is a reason why companies in every industry stay within their core competency and outsource the rest. I think this is why LinkedIn has discontinued various features, like Polls, Events, and Answers.

Third, there has been a trend in software development, especially web-based applications, where you develop the very best tool to accomplish A, B, or C and then find complementary tools to accomplish X, Y, Z. This allows multiple companies to share the burdens of designing, staying relevant, maintaining, etc. LinkedIn should be the very best application on which to find and be found and to portray your professional brand. It should find other systems that make up for its shortcomings and partner with, or acquire, them. You might refer to these as "mashups," of which there are thousands of examples. Here are a few:

- Many websites that require a login incorporate CAPTCHA technology. For example, if you leave a comment on a TypePad® blog, you'll likely have to type in the letters/numbers from an image to verify that you are a human being (and not an Internet robot).

- **Google Maps** integrates with sites to find sex offenders, bars, transit lines, or hundreds of other useful things.

- JibberJobber.com has mashups with various systems, including Google Maps to see your networks on a map, Skype to call a contact with one click, Copy2Contact to quickly capture email signatures and add them to your network, and Indeed.com to search multiple job boards from one interface.

In June 2007, LinkedIn announced they were going to follow Facebook's lead and allow third-party companies and individuals to create applications for LinkedIn users (similar to the mashup idea). There are millions of third-party Facebook apps. In a previous edition of this book, I wrote: "I'm guessing they are going to restrict access to a handful of strategic partners. I hope I'm proven wrong."

I wasn't wrong. Since LinkedIn Applications was announced, there have been very few third-party apps approved, and not much integration throughout the Internet. My company has requested permission to write apps to integrate with LinkedIn, but we haven't even heard back. This non-response is disheartening. It is clear they are definitely restricting their APIs to a handful of strategic partners. While disheartened, I think the restriction is good. Ultimately, any application you get from LinkedIn has its stamp of approval, or corporate endorsement. This means the app has probably gone through a vigorous quality assurance process, and the app creator can be trusted.

Chapter Summary

- LinkedIn is a powerful tool, but it is not a silver bullet.
- LinkedIn should be one component of your networking strategy, complemented with other tools.
- Different people use LinkedIn for different reasons—why do you use it?

"I'm a huge fan, user, and promoter of LinkedIn. I've used it to network into the technology field from print advertising and get my current job in a new high-growth department. Currently, a friend and I are founding an online apparel business. I've used LinkedIn to find manufacturers, screen printers, and as a resource for investors to research our management team."
Jimmy Hendricks, Cofounder and CEO, Deal Current,
http://www.dealcurrent.com

"So far, I primarily see my involvement on LinkedIn similar to having money in a savings account. It's not something I often tap, but something that's reassuring to have available when the need arises. I've also used LinkedIn as a journalist to make contact with people who might have expert knowledge on a topic."
Bernie Wagenblast, Editor, *Transportation Communications Newsletter*, http://transport-communications.blogspot.com/

"My favorite thing about LinkedIn is finding old contacts. I discovered an old college friend and several coworkers who moved on to other companies. It was nice to read about what they'd been up to in their profiles and reconnect."
Pete Johnson, Chief Architect, Hewlett-Packard,
http://www.hp.com/

"It's not about 'collecting and trading your friends' as I originally saw LinkedIn. It's really about visibility into relationships that you wouldn't know existed otherwise. The more people who know how to use the tool effectively, the more effective it is for everyone. What a terrific way to take your relationship to the next level!"
Scott Ingram, CEO and Founder, Network In Austin

3 Your Profile

This chapter talks about optimizing your profile to increase your chances of being found, and effectively communicate information about you.

In the early months of my job search, I was listening to a job coach teach a class about resumes, and he said something I thought was brilliant. I actually come back to this phrase regularly. He said, "Your resume is not your obituary, it is a marketing tool to get you into an interview." As a job seeker I could relate to this pull, even a sense of urgency, to put all of my work history and education on my resume. I was worried that leaving something off might mean they wouldn't get an interview or a job.

But the purpose of the resume is not to share all of the great things you've ever done. The resume is a marketing tool. Can you imagine a company's marketing tool telling the entire, long, detailed, and irrelevant story about their product? If a resume is a marketing tool, you should know who your customer (audience) is, and what message you want to leave with them. A marketing consultant might suggest that your marketing message has one, two, maybe three messages, but typically you don't want it to have more. More becomes confusing.

You should think of your LinkedIn profile the same way. Your profile is a marketing document, it is not your obituary, or brag sheet! When someone finds or reads your profile, you get a chance to market you, your products, and your services. If you have irrelevant clutter in your profile that is not important to your marketing message, you are only distracting the reader. The last thing a marketer wants to do is distract their audience!

Your profile should communicate your professional brand, including your relevant strengths, knowledge, and experience. Keep the message relevant to the role or services people are looking for, or relevant to the brand you are building. This means you need to identify your audience and what you want them to know about you. In light of that, here are some things to consider regarding your profile:

1. **How will old friends and people who knew you from your past find you?** Make sure you put names of schools, companies, and clubs in your profile. There is plenty of room to put a lot of this history in. You never know when that friend from five companies ago might search for you, and what opportunities she might present.

2. **How will recruiters, hiring managers, or potential business partners find you?** What search phrases will they put in when doing a search? Usually they aren't searching for your name, rather they would search for characteristics, skills or experience. They might search for the names of schools you attended or companies you have worked at. They might even search for company names that don't exist anymore, due to a merger or acquisition. Sometimes they might search for clubs or associations, especially if they were once members and have an affinity for the club or association. Recruiters look for candidates with specific experience, affiliations, work history, accomplishments, or network contacts. Include keywords and language you would have in a resume, so a recruiter looking for a "PHP programmer with CSS and Adobe experience," or a "project manager with a PMP near Washington, D.C." can be found. Many recruiters have had training on how to search for candidates on LinkedIn, and use various search techniques to find exactly what they are looking for, based on keywords, companies, etc.

3. **What first impression does your profile give?** You should spend at least as much time on your LinkedIn profile as you would on a resume or corporate marketing documentation. Whether you are looking for a job or not, you never know who is looking for you. After they find your profile, you want to be sure you leave a sharp first impression. Of course, you will have proper grammar and spelling in your profile. Beyond that, does your profile tell your story enough to engage me when I read it? Is it interesting, and do I walk away thinking, "This is the right person! My search is over!"

People may look for you based on things you have in common, like where you went to school. For example, let's say you attended UCLA.

You might have a classmate who has been looking for you, but can't remember your name. When he looks for other UCLA alumni, he might recognize your name or picture.

Unlike a resume, which is usually limited to two pages, a LinkedIn profile can be very, very long. Make sure the length of your profile doesn't take away from the marketing message. As long as everything in your profile is on-brand and on-message, you should be okay. Having a long profile and staying on-brand might seem at odds. How do you stay on-brand with a long profile? You would only work towards a long profile if you are trying to get more keywords, companies, etc. in your profile. Think about what your target contact would search for when looking for someone of your talent and make sure those keywords and phrases are peppered throughout your profile.

Many people think a LinkedIn profile is the new resume. I do not agree that a LinkedIn profile replaces a professional resume. I don't think anything is going to replace the traditional resume for quite a while because HR is very slow to change. The idea of something becoming an alternative to the resume has been a passionate conversation people have had for years. The beauty of sharing your LinkedIn profile is that it communicates much of the same information a resume communicates without sending the unspoken message of "I'm in a job search, can you help me?" Whether you are in an active transition or not, you can still let others know about you and what you have to offer. Many professionals who are not in transition have LinkedIn profiles.

A traditional resume has certain information including your job history, education, and skills. LinkedIn has sections for this information and more. Here are some differences between a LinkedIn profile and a traditional resume:

1. LinkedIn doesn't allow bulleted formatting. You can get around this with a trick, but it still isn't the regular bullet formatting that we're used to. Because a profile doesn't have bullets, people tend to write in a paragraph narrative format, without the typical "quantification" you see on a resume. You should include proof of your skills and value, even explaining how valuable you have been in past roles. For example, on a resume you would include statements like "increased department revenues by 150 percent and profits by 250 percent in 18 months." I recommend you include that information in your LinkedIn profile, but you don't have to do it with the same dry language you might have in a resume. Include quantitative results and back it up with on-brand language in a narrative. The example above might be rewritten as follows: "I am known to bring quick significant value to the top and bottom line of companies I work for. In a recent role as

product manager, I increased department revenues by 150 percent and profits by 250 percent in 18 months."

2. Your LinkedIn profile can be richer than a resume, with embedded files, rich media, links to other value-add pages, and more. In the most recent profile makeover, LinkedIn introduced sections to put information about projects, certifications, publications, and more. These can be mentioned in a resume, but in a LinkedIn profile you get a lot of room to really expound your background and value.

3. If you are a member of LinkedIn groups, or follow companies or "influencers," these will (by default) show up on your profile. This gives the viewer unusual insight into your interests. I've seen profiles where the person is following all of their competitors, which is cool for them, but they aren't as discreet as they probably think they are.

As I mentioned earlier, one of the most important considerations while creating your profile is making it easy for people to find you. This is usually done with keywords in the right places. Fortunately, your profile is indexed by search engines such as Yahoo! and Google, which means that optimizing your profile for searches will benefit you, whether people are looking for you in LinkedIn or on a search engine.

There is a common phrase amongst Internet marketers called "search engine optimization" (SEO). The idea behind SEO is that you are trying to optimize a web page (or in this case, your LinkedIn profile) so search engines bring it up first, or in the first page of search results). Optimize your LinkedIn profile with SEO in mind. Here are some tricks you can incorporate as you develop your profile:

1. **School names**—Include the full name (University of Virginia) as well as the common abbreviation (UVA).

2. **Company names**—Just as you did with the school names, make sure you put the official and common names of the companies where you worked. If your company is a subsidiary of a larger company, put the name of the larger company also. That way if a recruiter is looking for someone from either the main company or the subsidiary, they are more likely to come across your profile.

3. **Technical skills**—A recruiter might look for "project managers" or someone who is a "project manager professional," and they might search for "PMP" or someone who is a member of the "PMI" (Project Management Institute). Put all of those alternatives.

4. **Keywords**—Include keywords used to describe your skills, abilities, or professional passions. I've found that putting the keyword in your current title increases your SEO, and it seems that the number of occurrences of a keyword (or key phrase) improves your SEO.

Aside from writing your profile so the search engine finds you, write it so the person reading your profile is impressed by the value you bring to a potential relationship. Deb Dib, The CEO Coach, wrote a powerful article for CEOs titled "LinkedIn—What It Is and Why You Need to Be On It."[7] Check out the eight profiles she links to in that article, which are all examples of excellent LinkedIn profiles, whether you are a CEO or not!

TIP: Lonny Gulden, a recruiter in Minnesota, suggests including company names from any company you worked at but has since changed its name (perhaps due to a merger or acquisition). Recruiters might look for ex-employees of those defunct companies because of the training or experience they had at past companies.

I've seen many profiles through the years. When I critique a profile, I typically look at many things, including:

1. **Name:** Is it just your name or does it include superfluous information like a phone number, email address, or credentials and acronyms? With few exceptions, the name field should just include your name, without anything else.

2. **Picture:** I recommend a close-up of a headshot that looks professional. The picture should make your profile more personable. Too many pictures are not zoomed in enough, or have too many distractions, whether conflicting colors or a busy background.

3. **Professional headline:** This is YOUR CHANCE to share your value proposition. Don't just put title/company, like so many people do. Tell me what value you bring to me (or, to your client or prospect). This is one of the first lines someone sees when they come to your profile.

4. **Current title:** Critical for when someone searches for you by profession. You might put in alternative titles, even if it isn't your official title (only do this honestly, even if you have to include an explanation of not having that exact title, but you have the role and responsibilities of the title).

5. **Vanity URL:** Edit your Public Profile URL so it has your name, or something more deliberate, perhaps something with your job title or professional experience.

7. **Summary:** Use as many of the two thousand characters you can get in the summary as possible. Write an engaging narrative! You

---

7. http://www.job-hunt.org/executive-job-search/linkedin-for-executives.shtml

can use Problem, Action, Results (PAR) statements to strengthen your claims. For example, you might say "I am known as a team player. For example," and then put in a story with the PAR format. Spend time on the Summary; tell engaging stories and put keywords in the right places.

8. **Experience and education:** Treat this the same as the Summary. This is another opportunity to include keywords for SEO, as well as stories and supportive brand messaging. The more you fill in this 2,000 character opportunity with stories and keywords, the stronger your profile will be.

9. **Interests:** Below the recommendations section is the interests section—yet another area to freehand more information, branding, and SEO words.

10. **Groups and associations:** ONLY show groups that are supportive of your brand. You don't need to show all groups you are a member of—only show those that support your brand.

11. **Contact settings:** This is an excellent place to put something like, "The best way to contact me is via email at Jason@JibberJobber.com," or something like that. This helps people contact you even if they aren't connected to you. I always look for contact information on a profile when I do critiques because I'm looking for an easy way to get in touch with a prospect. Make it easy for people to communicate with you, without the need to upgrade.

Once you create a strong profile, you don't have to worry about revisiting it to keep it up to date. Of course, you should keep it updated with relevant changes, but most people can easily go a year or two (or more) without updating their profile. Scott Allen, a social marketing expert, shared a story on his blog[8] about a timely profile update that resulted in $5,000 of additional revenue. A simple way to get value out of frequent updates is to change your title (only as appropriate), which is a simple way you can push your information to the email inbox of your contacts.

Your "public profile" is what people see if they are not logged into LinkedIn. It's important to think about what is visible and what is hidden. In the settings page you'll find a link to edit your public profile. This page allows you to choose what you show and hide to people who are not logged in.

---

8. http://linkedintelligence.com/the-5000-profile-update/

Supposedly, these options allow you to choose the degree of privacy you are comfortable with. I have two thoughts on this:

> **First,** you should provide as much information as possible, so visitors who find your profile can get the gist of who you are and what you have to offer, without having to login (or worse, create a new account, and then login).

> **Second,** consider your personal comfort level regarding privacy. If you are comfortable putting up certain information on your regular, non-public profile, which is available to over two hundred sixty million people, why not let non-LinkedIn people see it? It doesn't make sense to hide anything from people who are not logged into LinkedIn, especially if you put stuff up that reinforces your brand.

The purpose of a profile is to showcase who you are in a professional setting, not to record private data. It's great to be concerned about privacy, but with the technology available today, there are dozens of places someone can go to find your personal information, including your contact information, professional and work history, home address and telephone number, even your social security number! My recommendation is to click every box in the public profile settings and let everyone see what you put on your LinkedIn profile.

Having a strong and well-crafted profile gives you the opportunity to communicate your brand, abilities, and professional goals. The alternative is to let search engines determine that for you. Don't you want more control over your brand and messaging, than whatever random thing a search engine shows? Your profile, and the ability to be found by people who are looking for you, is central to your success with LinkedIn, so make sure you spend enough time and effort to get it right.

In late 2012 and early 2013, LinkedIn rolled out the biggest change to the LinkedIn profile that we have ever seen. The updates allow us to have a richer profile that we have more control over. Here are the things that you should do, or need to know, about the new profile:

1. The profile picture is now shown in a bigger space. If you had a picture just for the size of the image they used to have, you should upload a bigger picture. Otherwise, your picture will be surrounded by a thick gray border.

2. At the top of your profile, there is not a line for titles anymore, which gave context to your companies. Companies have less meaning without an accompanying title The main way to communicate your value-add now is through the professional headline. This was once

quite important. Now that it's the only branding statement you see before scrolling down, it's significantly more important than it ever was.

3. Many of the sections below the heading can be reordered by dragging-and-dropping. This allows you to put the most valuable information towards the top of your profile.

4. There is a new "activities" section that adds zero value. In my opinion, it is a distraction. I suggest you go into your settings and show the activities to "only you," so no one else gets this distraction.

5. The summary and work experience sections allow you to upload rich media, including PowerPoints, documents, and audio/video. Make use of this awesome addition to the profile by putting rich media everywhere you can!

6. There are various new sections for the profile including publications, projects, organization, honors & awards, test scores, patents, etc. Use these to enhance your SEO and increase your chance of being found, but don't clutter your profile with information that is off-brand or distracting. If you put those in, use stories to enhance your expertise and professional passions.

7. If you have blogs or write articles, put those in the publications section. This replaces the three websites that we used to be able to add to our profile. Putting links to your blogs and other written works in publications is awesome because you can write much more about those sites than you used to be able to.

8. I am completely disenchanted with the skills and endorsements section. An endorsement is practically meaningless. However, I predict LinkedIn will make endorsements more important by having the number of endorsements impact search results. If and when that happens, we'll all be fishing for more endorsements.

9. Your profile shows what companies and influencers you are following. I don't think anyone can really mess this up, just realize that when you follow a company or influencer, others can see that.

When you make changes to your LinkedIn profile, consider going into settings and turning off any broadcast of changes.

The strongest profiles I see have a fair amount of keywords. There is confusion on exactly how many you need to put, and where, but what I've found is that you want to have a lot. Here's how you figure out how many you should have: do a search for your specialty, for example, product manager. Go into the top five or ten profiles that come up and count the number of times that word or phrase is in their profile. The

I'm on LinkedIn—Now What???

easiest way to do that is to hit Control-F on your keyboard to open the "find" dialog on your browser, and then type the word or phrase in. You'll get a count very quickly. If the top five or ten profiles have thirty or more instances of the word or phrase, you should have at least that many.

In addition to the number of times a word or phrase is repeated, I've found that putting the word or phrase in certain places gives it more weight. For example, if you put "product manager" in all of your titles, that seems to be better than just mentioning it in the description of the job.

In the descriptions of jobs and in the summary, you should have PAR statements, as I mentioned above. Another thing I love to see is use of recommendations you've received. I don't necessarily want to see an entire recommendation in your summary, but I would love to see something like this: "People tend to say I am..." and then use a phrase or line from a recommendation you've received.

Instead of saying that you are a great team player, you could say "engineers I work with tend to say they want me on their team. They say my analytical skills are..." and then continue with phrases from recommendations. Put these statements in quotes, and you can even say, "For more, scroll down to see my recommendations." It's always more powerful to have someone else talk about you than for you to talk about yourself.

Chapter Summary

- Set up your profile as completely as possible so that others have a better chance of finding you.

- Make sure you check spelling, grammar, and overall readability of your profile. This is not just for the search engine, but for the human who reads your profile.

- Take advantage of things such as the Vanity URL and Recommendations to make your profile look stronger and more professional.

- Allow others to see all of the information on your Public Profile.

"I'm starting to think LinkedIn may be Resume 2.0, but I'm not 100 percent convinced yet. When I beefed up my profile, I actually copied and pasted bullet points from my latest conventional resume, and now that thing is searchable for all the world to see. That's a lot different than posting it in some random place on a few job sites. It's in a neutral place where you expect pressure-reduced interactions with others."
Pete Johnson, Chief Architect, Hewlett-Packard,
http://www.hp.com

"When you set up your profile, make sure it's a snapshot—no one wants to read a detailed autobiography. And don't forget to proofread!"
Christine Dennison, Job Search Expert, Dennison Career Services, http://www.thejobsearchcoach.com

"Your LinkedIn profile is a critical part of your online identity. Make sure to complete it with information that conveys what you do, the value you deliver, and the audience you serve; in other words, have it reflect your personal brand."
Walter Akana, Life Strategist, Threshold Consulting,
http://www.threshold-consulting.com

"I think the status update feature is one of the coolest things on the LinkedIn profile! Used strategically and well, the status update line can be used to promote your business, products, and personal brand to your network. I use it to promote my blog posts, speaking engagements, and networking events or conferences I'm attending to facilitate the possibility of connecting in person or on the Web with those in my network. As a recruiter, I also use the status update to make my network aware of opportunities that I'm recruiting for. I have a fairly large network—over 1,500 connections—so that's 1,500+ opportunities to reach candidates or get referrals—and it works! I also encourage job seekers to use the status update feature to make sure their network knows that they are currently searching for a new opportunity. Regularly updating your status keeps you on 'top of mind' and on the homepage of those in your network."
Jennifer McClure, Executive Recruiter/Executive Coach; and President, Unbridled Talent, LLC, http://unbridledtalent.com

I'm on LinkedIn—Now What???

4 Account, Privacy, & Settings

There is a "Privacy & Settings" link under the dropdown you see when you mouse over your picture, at the top right of every page.

This section of LinkedIn has one of the most important menus in LinkedIn. This is where you can determine what messages you get via email. You can see what you get at your current account level and what you would get if you upgrade. I have a "basic" account, and I see I have five Introductions available and no InMails.

It looks like there are thirteen different types of accounts: the free Basic account that everyone starts off with, three additional levels for recruiters, three levels for job seekers, three levels for sales professionals, and three levels for anyone who wants something different. The lowest price is $15.95/month, although most levels are between $19 and $99/month. You can see a comparison chart showing pricing and features when you click on an upgrade link or button. One way to get there is to click on the Privacy and Settings dropdown, and then click on the yellow Upgrade button.

I have found the basic (free) account to be fine for almost everyone I talk to and consult with. I generally suggest you learn the tricks to get around the limitations of the free account, rather than pay for an upgrade. For example, in an upgraded account, you can see more results in the search for people. Instead of upgrading and getting triple the results, I suggest you learn how to refine your search criteria and get better results that are more relevant to you. Learning to search better can save you hundreds of dollars each year, and you'll have less irrelevant results to sift through.

Who would benefit from an upgraded account? Anyone who uses LinkedIn for hours each month to find people and try and communicate with them. Recruiter and sales professionals are prospecting all the time, and trying to reach out to people who are 3rd degree contacts. Some job seekers who are looking for higher-level positions, and doing a lot of prospecting on LinkedIn, might find value in an upgrade.

If you don't spend much time on LinkedIn, don't use the search tool much, or don't need to use LinkedIn's InMail communication tool with people you aren't connected with, you will likely be fine with a free account. If you figure out how to do more relevant searches and communicate with people outside of InMail, you don't need the upgrade. Many people have enough contact information on their Profile, or their contact information is accessible in Google search results, that you don't need to use InMail. I've had a free account for years, and it's been fine for my needs.

NOTE: Shortly before LinkedIn went public, they started to move features that were once in the free level to the premium level. One change was no longer allowing you to see details of a third-degree contact, unless they had certain privacy settings opened up. Make sure your privacy settings aren't keeping you from being seen, and figure out ways to see other people's information (by joining a Group they are in, or by doing an X-ray search (see Chapter 6).

Settings is one of the most important places to visit if you feel like you get too much or too little correspondence (emails) from LinkedIn. There are different functions in LinkedIn that can send communications to you. For example, if someone wants to get in touch with you, they might be able to figure out how to message you through LinkedIn's communication system. If someone starts a discussion in a LinkedIn group, and you are in that group, LinkedIn will likely send you an email with that discussion and other active discussions from the group. If someone updates their title, you might get a message from LinkedIn. This is kind of cool, but it can be overwhelming, depending on how many contacts you have and how many groups you are in. If your contacts are salespeople or recruiters, you might be bombarded with messages that are not relevant to you. No one needs more messages cluttering up their email inbox, right?

The default settings (of sending me a lot of emails) did not meet my needs and might not meet yours. I was getting more emails than I wanted from LinkedIn. Combine this with the messages I was getting from Facebook, Yahoo! Groups, and other networks and systems and you can imagine how my efforts to manage my "information overload" were failing.

Frustrated by too many notifications, I finally went to my settings section and changed the default settings, so now I only get what I want in my email inbox. All of the messages are still available, if I want to see them, in my LinkedIn Inbox. I'm not limiting my ability to get messages; I'm simply choosing whether I get them via email or in my LinkedIn Inbox.

This is how I have some of my settings (most of the others are set to not send me emails):

- **Introductions and InMails**—I get these via email, so if someone tries to get in touch with me, I won't miss their message. The LinkedIn landing page is too cluttered for me to read every single message I get, and I don't want these types of messages to get lost. I also don't use LinkedIn's Inbox to manage any of my messages, and don't want to have to go there to find them.

- **Invitations**—I also have invitations sent to my email inbox. An invitation comes from someone who wants to join my network and could be an important new relationship, or an important offline relationship that is ready to connect online.

- **Job suggestions**—These are job openings that come from people in my network. I thought it would be useful to get these notifications and pass leads to friends who are in transition. Unfortunately, I got so many irrelevant job notifications sent to me, it became overwhelming. This was the most prevalent communication I got from LinkedIn, which prompted me to check out and manage my email settings. I quickly changed this setting from "Individual Email" to "No Email."

The options in this section change every once in a while. While doing the research for this book, I found there are new settings to check based on a recent acquisition of LinkedIn. If you find yourself getting too many emails from LinkedIn, simply go to the Communications tab of your account page, and click on "Set the frequency of emails" to see if there are new settings you need to change.

Under the profile settings tab is the option to "select who can see your connections." This used to be the "Connections Browse" option, which was under the privacy controls. This has always been a controversial option, and for good reason. You can choose to show your first-degree connections to your first-degree contacts, or you can hide them.

To me, hiding your connections seems to contradict what LinkedIn is about: the ability to see who is in one another's network! However, the option is a privacy setting and I've heard from people who have needed that level of supposed privacy. Perhaps they were in a bad relationship, or they have a stalker, and they want to close down access to their contacts. This is a legitimate reason to not share your contacts with others. Why do I say "supposed privacy?" Even if you choose to hide your connections with this setting, your first-degree contacts can still see who you are connected to!

For example, let's say you have a first-degree contact who is a project manager in Seattle. When I search for "project manager" or "Seattle," I will see everyone in my first three degrees (including your first- and second-degree contacts), **even** if you have said I can't "see" your connections. You aren't precluding me from seeing your contacts, you are simply making it a little harder for me to see them, particularly in a nice list of just your contacts. Again, don't presume much privacy.

Another critical setting has to do with your email address(es). I encourage you to make sure you have the right email addresses associated with your account. I have two email addresses I use: one for the business I own (my work email) and another through Gmail (my personal email). I send a lot of emails every day, some from my work account and others from my personal account. I make it easy for people to use either address when they invite me to connect. Why? Some of my contacts only know me from my personal account, while others know me from my work account. LinkedIn allows potential contacts to send me an invitation to connect using either address.

I think it is essential you use an email address you own, and have complete control over, as the primary email address. Over the years, we have seen articles and email threads where the discussion was based around a person growing their LinkedIn network while working at their job, with the employer claiming the network belonged to the company. This is an interesting claim. I can see why the employer claims the LinkedIn account and network connections as theirs, but I think it puts the employee in a poor position. After all, it is a human-to-human relationship. Furthermore, I know of at least one employer who terminated an employee, and then used the "forgot email" tool to change the password and the entire account (including the profile), while having complete access to the network.

To avoid losing your contacts and all of your hard work, make sure you control the email addresses on your account, especially the primary address. You can get free email accounts from Hotmail, Yahoo!, Gmail, and a host of other providers. Make sure your primary address is one of these, not an address from your employer, even if you own the company.

Here's a summary of some of my settings:

Setting Name	How I've Set My Account
Introductions and InMails	Email me immediately
Invitations	Email me immediately
Job notifications	No email; I'll look on the website
Who can see my connections	Allow my connections to see my connections
Email addresses	My Gmail account is the primary address, my JibberJobber account is a secondary address

Chapter Summary

- Dive into the settings pages to set up your preferences — this will determine when you receive emails and when you don't!

- If you have multiple email addresses, make sure you put them in your account-that way, others can connect with you by sending an invitation to either email account. Never use an employer-sponsored email as your primary email on record.

- Not allowing your contacts to see your other contacts will prevent them from seeing the complete list of all of your first-degree contacts, but it does not block those contacts from showing up in search results.

"Learn the site. There is a lot of useful help listed under Help & FAQ. If you take the time to review your account and settings, and set your account up properly, your time on LinkedIn will be much easier."
Sheilah Etheridge, Owner, SME Management,
http://www.linkedin.com/in/smemanagement

5 Connecting with Others

Central to your LinkedIn experience, and your success with it, is how and when to connect with other people. Consider a spectrum where one end represents people who are open networkers—they accept any invitation they get and freely extend invitations to anyone they can. On the other end of the spectrum, are people who are more conservative about whom they connect with—this is the closed networker.

I can't tell you what kind of networker you should be. This is an individual decision for each person, and I've found there isn't a "right" answer that everyone should adopt. Depending on your circumstances, you might choose to change your connection strategy over time. In this chapter, we'll talk about considerations regarding the open/closed spectrum concept. I'll explain characteristics of both ends of the spectrum and give you enough information to decide what your own connection policy should be.

Open Networking

Open networkers are those who connect with anyone, no matter what. You may have heard of the LinkedIn LION, which is an acronym that stands for "LinkedIn Open Networker." I wrote a blog post titled "I'm a LION—Hear Me ROAR"[9] that got a number of interesting comments. LIONs are

---

9. http://imonlinkedinnowwhat.com/2008/07/31/im-a-lion-hear-me-roar/

interested in having as many connections as they can get. Declaring you are a LION indicates you are willing to accept an invitation from anyone.

Not every LION is really an open networker, and not every open networker is a LION. Open networkers tend to subscribe to the theory that having more connections means you have more channels, or ability, to reach a key person. This might be true (I'll share my personal connection philosophy at the end of this chapter), but I'm not convinced spending a lot of time haphazardly growing your network is a good use of time.

Why would you want to be an open networker? Having a large number of first-degree contacts can give you richer search results and allow you to communicate with more people through LinkedIn.

For example, a recruiter wants to have access to "passive candidates" (people who are not active job seekers). If she has one hundred first-degree contacts in LinkedIn, she might find the right candidate for a job she's trying to fill. Imagine she has four thousand first-degree connections. Don't you think it's more likely she finds the right candidates when she searches through her bigger network? A search returns first -, second-, and third -degree contacts, so every new first-degree contact you make brings their network to you, making your pool of contacts searched much larger. This is why many recruiters on LinkedIn are "open networkers."

I used a recruiter for the previous example, but there are other professions that find open networking beneficial. If you are in a role where you actively look for people, or try to reach out to people, you would likely benefit from an open networking strategy. Some professions who would benefit from such a strategy include salespeople, business development people, entrepreneurs, or other power connectors. "Power connector" is an expression I was introduced to when I read Keith Ferrazzi's *Never Eat Alone* book. He uses this brilliant phrase to describe people who are very powerful networkers, and help many others with introductions.

Open networkers can quickly and easily grow their personal LinkedIn networks by downloading the Outlook toolbar and inviting all of their Outlook connections to join LinkedIn. In addition, you can import your contact lists from online email accounts, such as Yahoo!, AOL, Hotmail, and Gmail.

I DO NOT RECOMMEND DOING THIS, even if you are a LION.

Instead, I recommend that you prepare your contacts to connect with you outside of LinkedIn, before you invite them through LinkedIn. In other words, ask them if they'd accept an invitation to connect in an email, over the phone, face-to-face, etc. before you send an invitation to connect.

Historically, each user was limited to sending out three thousand invitations. I've never reached this limit, but I'm regularly asked about it. If you use your three thousand invitations, simply request more from LinkedIn customer service. I understand additional invitations are granted in blocks of one hundred.

There is justified confusion amongst LinkedIn users about whether LinkedIn encourages you to be an open networker or to be a closed networker. In the past, someone you invited could have clicked a button that said, "I don't know" you. If five people clicked that, your account would have been penalized. This button is not there anymore, but many people are still gun-shy about whom they invite. LinkedIn says to only connect with people you "know and trust," but they give you the import tools to connect with everyone in your address book. Only a small percentage of my contacts in my address books are people I know or trust. So should I do what they say, or should I use the tools they give me? It can be confusing.

Closed Networking

On the other end of the open/closed networker spectrum, are the closed networkers. Closed networkers are those who only connect with those they "know and trust," abiding by LinkedIn's recommendation. Instead of accepting every single connection request, closed networkers will evaluate the relationship with the person requesting the connection, and only connect when they feel comfortable to do so. I know people who will only connect with you if they have met you in person and spent time with you.

Is it bad to be a closed networker? Not necessarily. There is value in knowing the people you are connected with. You can give more of your connections a recommendation than an open networker can, because you actually know them. You are more likely to get real recommendations from your contacts. You can feel comfortable making introductions or passing introduction requests on, because you know all of the parties in the introduction. Closed networkers value the individual relationship with each connection they have, and treat LinkedIn as less of a database to find new contacts than do open networkers.

Many people who are closed networkers on LinkedIn are open net-workers in a more general sense. They will have more relaxed standards on other social networking sites, or they network in person. Many closed networkers use LinkedIn the way it was designed to be used, but might not get as much value out of their extended network as an open networker could.

The Canned Invitation

Another topic that gets a lot of attention is how to ask someone to connect with you. The default invitation that LinkedIn provides can be cheesy and impersonal. You can change it, but you have to remember to do so—and it's easy to forget! For as long as I can remember, the default invitation has been:

I'd like to add you to my professional network on LinkedIn.

Every blog post I've read regarding the default invitation is negative. Every LinkedIn consultant recommends you make the invitation personal. I totally agree! Leaving the invitation content as scanned text is like saying, "I don't care about you—you are just a number to me."

When I invite someone to connect in LinkedIn, I change the default invitation so the recipient knows (or remembers) who I am, and they can get the feeling that I am serious about a professional relationship.

Incorporate your style in the invitations you send through LinkedIn. Whether your style is more casual or more formal, your personality definitely has a place in your online communications.[10]

The best invitations I receive are concise and include the following information:

- **Here's who I am.** This is not a time to brag or list all of your wonderful skills and experiences. There isn't room to do that, and if your invitation is too long, I probably won't read it. Instead, let me know something about you without making me look at your profile. Give our potential relationship context.

- **Here's how I came across your profile.** Did you find me in a LinkedIn search? Did you meet me at a networking event or find me on a Yahoo! Group? Let me know how you found me, so I don't have to wonder if I'm just a number to you.

- **Here's why I'd like to connect.** You don't HAVE TO have a reason to connect, other than just wanting to connect and get to know one another better. However, if you tell me why you want to connect, I'll be able to determine what next steps might be. Every relationship starts somewhere. If you have a specific reason to connect, let me know what it is, and let me know how we can move towards that.

---

10. http://linkedintelligence.com/better-boilerplates/

There are even cheesier ways to invite someone to connect than the default invitation that LinkedIn provides, and I see it regularly. Some people make equally ambiguous invitation messages and use them as their canned copy-and-paste messages, time and again. They don't customize their canned message to include anything specific to OUR relationship. They replace one canned invitation with another canned invitation.

If someone invites you to connect, and they use the canned invitation, I suggest you be forgiving. I have invited people to connect by clicking a button on LinkedIn, thinking it would then allow me to customize the invitation, but it didn't. It simply sent the invitation to connect once I clicked the button. Give your contact the benefit of the doubt and focus on starting the relationship right, instead of thinking they are networking rookies not worthy of your time.

YOUR Connection Strategy

The open/closed spectrum is just that: a spectrum. You might not be on either extreme, as defined above. Most people tend to sit somewhere in the middle. I won't say you are right or wrong in your decision, because it is a personal choice.

In *The Virtual Handshake*, the authors talk about ensuring you have diversity in your network. Think about what that means. If you are an accountant, connected only with other accountants, you don't have diversity. What kind of professionals do accountants work with? CFOs, CEOs, accounting vendors, tax professionals, HR professionals, IT professionals, and more. See the diversity that accountants could have in their networks if they connected with a few people from each of those groups? What types of professionals should you include in your network?

In addition to adding diversity to your network with other types of professions (think job titles), add diversity with other industries. What contacts could you connect with from complementary industries? Think about your industry and who serves you. Who are your vendors and service providers? Think about whom they work with, and clients that are in other industries. We cross-pollinate a lot in our daily work, and cross-pollinating between professions and industries could add value to your online networking.

As you diversify your first-degree network, you should see a remarkable difference in your second- and third–degree contacts. This should give you more interesting search results, and let you tap into a different type of network than if everyone had a similar job title to yours.

Another element of diversity in your network is geography. Where are your connections? Do you do business locally, regionally, nationally, or internationally? You should have a significant amount of contacts based on where your geographic interests are. For example, if you do a lot of business in Seattle or Florida, get a lot of contacts in Seattle or Florida. Grow your network where your clients and prospects are, even if the new contacts are not in your industry or profession.

Final Thoughts Regarding Connections

Issues surrounding invitations and connections are well debated. Some people are offended by those who don't share their views on how to use LinkedIn to network. Others pass judgment on those who have different styles, even though their objectives may be different.

Awareness of how others use LinkedIn and where they lie on the open/closed spectrum will help you understand why they may accept or reject a connection invitation, how they react to your request for an introduction, or how they invite you. One of the most frequent questions I get is, "If I disconnect from someone, will they get a notice?" No one gets a notice when you disconnect from them, so feel free to clean up your network as often as you wish.

Chapter Summary

- There are pros and cons to open and closed networking strategies—you need to determine what's best for you.

- When you invite someone to connect, be sensitive how you come across, and customize the invitation message when appropriate.

- Change your connection strategy as needed, and respect the strategies that others have chosen.

"LinkedIn works best when you use it with focused outcomes in mind. I am always open to invitations, but take a look at my profile first and tell me why you are interested in connecting with me. A little 'wooing' goes a long way!"
Garland Coulson, The EBusiness Tutor; and Founder, Free Traffic Bar, http://garlandcoulson.com

"I asked people to join my network due to their 'status'...what a mistake. Invite only people you trust, regardless of their position or status."
David Armstrong, Founder, Bounce Base,
http://davidarmstrong.me

"Most of my LinkedIn contacts come through an electronic newsletter I edit that's focused on the transportation industry. I sent an invitation to the subscribers who were already part of LinkedIn to connect with me. I see it as one more way readers of the newsletter might gain value from being subscribers. Since the subscriber list is private, those who are part of my LinkedIn network can see others who are part of my network and make a connection, either directly or through me."
Bernie Wagenblast, Editor, *Transportation Communications Newsletter*, http://transport-communications.blogspot.com/

"I wasted several InMails and Introductions when I could have simply hit the 'Add [contact name] to your Network' button because I thought I had to know their current emails to use that. I think this is very common."
Ingo Dean, Senior Manager of Global IT, Virage Logic,
http://www.linkedin.com/in/ingodean

"Be open to a diverse network. You never know whom you can help or who can help you. It's OK if you only want known people in your network, or only people from one industry, etc. But the more diverse your network is, the more rewarding it can be. This is especially true if you want to gain business from the site. People in your industry most likely won't need your services, but those in other industries may."
Sheilah Etheridge, Owner, SME Management,
http://www.linkedin.com/in/smemanagement

"Links to people can be broken—if you connected to a person that is suddenly sending you a boatload of spam just because you're 'LinkedIn buddies,' you can (and should) break the link."
Phil Gerbyshak, Author, *10 Ways to Make It Great!*; Owner, The Make It Great Guy, http://www.philgerbyshak.com/

"I hate receiving a LinkedIn 'invitation to connect' template. They lack authenticity and make me feel the person does not value the relationship enough to compose a personalized message. Take the time to create a touch point with your contact…it is well worth the extra effort."
Barbara Safani, Owner, Career Solvers,
http://www.careersolvers.com

Part II
Making It Work for You

Now that you have your profile and account settings set up, let's get into the proactive part of LinkedIn. In Part II we'll talk about what it means to connect with other LinkedIn users, how to find relevant contacts, what "degrees of separation" is, how to give and accept recommendations, how to use LinkedIn Jobs (even if you aren't in a job search), and how LinkedIn Groups could benefit you.

6 Finding Contacts

Searching for contacts on LinkedIn was my first great frustration. I had fewer than five people in my network when I searched for management jobs in Utah. I was totally surprised to see no results on this simple and general search! This chapter talks about having a better search experience than I had, as well as how to find relevant contacts outside the search box.

Here's what I've learned since those early days when I had only five connections:

Increase the size of your network. If you are interested in people and opportunities in your city, look for more local connections. If you are interested in people and opportunities in your industry or profession, expand your LinkedIn network with industry and professional contacts. As your network grows with relevant connections, you are more likely to get relevant search results. Your search results are based on your connections. Here is a key concept I teach with regard to growing your network: grow your network with RELEVANT contacts. The more relevant your contacts are (regardless of how strong your relationship is with them), the more relevant your search results should be.

Connect with a few super-connectors. Super-connectors are LinkedIn users who have many connections, usually in the thousands. Connecting with super-connectors significantly increases your visibility in the system. These connections enhance your ability to find (because you have access to their network) and to be found (because their connections are likely doing searches, and now you are a second-degree contact to the super-connector). You don't have to connect with very many super-connectors. Some of them are general connectors, while others might be highly relevant to you, based on their location, profession, or industry. Connecting with even two or three super-connectors could give you a significant boost in visibility and greater reach. As you connect with super-connectors, try to get to know them. Learn how you can add value to them, and become more than just another connection. Also, look for super-connecters with networks that are relevant to you.

Use the basic search forms. It is easy to overlook the basic search tool in LinkedIn, but it should be a significant part of your user experience. The search form allows you to search people, jobs, companies, groups, universities, and even your LinkedIn inbox, using whatever keywords you want. Try a few searches based on industry or professional keywords, perhaps words that are on your resume, or that are in a job opening you are interested in, and see what comes up. You'll likely find some new potential contacts to reach out to. You might see some profiles with information that you want to borrow for your own profile.

Understand advanced search options. Usually the quick search allows you to find what you're looking for. However, there is significant power in the advanced search page. Scott Allen has talked about using LinkedIn to fill your spare time on business trips by meeting new contacts you find through LinkedIn. He suggests you search for people in the city you will be in, which you can do with the advanced search.

Choose the country and zip code filter (which is only available if you are in certain countries, including the United States, Canada, and United Kingdom). If you are an international traveler you won't always be able to do a zip or postal code search, but you should be able to use the country name to narrow your search.

Here are some of the useful features in the advanced search form:

Keywords—This could be a company name, a technology, the name of a certification, a club or school, or a person's first or last name. A search here is the same as using the simple search at the top of any page. Note that if you want to get results based on a company name, you should put that name in the Company field. On the advanced search, use as many of the boxes as you can to be more specific before using the Keywords box.

Title—This is one of the most important advanced search boxes. When I was in my job search, I wanted to network with "CEOs," "managers," and "project managers." Since I've been in a sales role with my company, I've looked for "career center directors," "career coaches," "resume writers," people who work in outplacement, and other career professionals. I leave all other fields blank and then fill in the Title box with an appropriate title for a prospect, and choose to limit the search to current titles only (the option from the drop-down menu below the titles field).

Company—Use this field to do company research as you prepare to network into a company, or research competitors or an industry. Try various versions of a company name (e.g., GE and General Electric), as well as names of subsidiaries, competitors, etc. You can limit the results to current companies only, or search for current and past companies, the same way you can with titles.

Location—Choose the country (and zip or postal code, if possible). I would use the local search option with other search criteria, such as "project manager" in Seattle (you'll need the zip code). This is a powerful way to find contacts that are local to you, are in the same city you're traveling to, or are in the industry you are trying to prospect into.

Industry—If you don't know who you are looking for, but know what industry you want to target, this is a great search. Leave all of the search fields blank and select the industry you are interested in.

School—I did a search on one of my alma maters and got different results when I used the school acronym (BYU: 1,454 results) than I did when I used the full name (Brigham Young University: 81,690 results). There are two lessons here. First, when you are searching for people by school, try it both ways. Second, make sure you have both versions in your profile. Unless you are using other search criteria (like name, title, etc.), I encourage you to check out LinkedIn.com/alumni, which is a relatively new view that gives you really interesting insight into where people at a university have ended up and what they are doing.

NOTE: Any search criteria with a gold/orange LinkedIn icon is not available unless you upgrade. I suggest you try in-depth searching with the free fields before considering an upgrade.

The bigger your network, and the better connected they are (do they each have five connections, or do they each have fifty or more connections?), the better your results you should be. As I mentioned earlier, the more contacts you have that are relevant to you (based on geography, profession and industry), the more relevant your search results will be.

You can also incorporate Boolean criteria into your searches. This means you can use AND, OR, and NOT; quotes ("product manager" instead of product manager); and parenthesis. For example, try any of the following searches in the Advanced Search page (you can put these in the Keywords or Company or Title fields), or the simple search box at the top of any page:

- Google NOT Microsoft (I got 294,281 results)

- Microsoft NOT Google (I got 101,719 results)

- Google AND Microsoft (I got 2,773 results)

- php -programmer -linux -javascript -css +html -mysql (a "+" means it has to include the phrase, "-" means the profile cannot include the phrase)

- project management institute" (use quotes for an exact match of the term)

- "project management institute" AND (Microsoft OR SUN); (combine term in quotes, parenthesis, and AND/OR operators for very specific results)

Combinations of these tricks will be enough for most people. For more in-depth information on really advanced searching, steal some tricks from Google's search tips page.[11]

One of the techniques that recruiters and savvy prospectors use is called x-ray searching. I'll let Glen Cathey, a master of this technique, teach you more on his blog, BooleanBlackBelt.com. He has done extensive research on different ways to construct an x-ray search and how these compare with searching from with LinkedIn.

The basic premise of an x-ray search is using a search engine's ability to return results from only one website. For example, in Google you can do a search on just LinkedIn by putting this in the search box:

site:linkedin.com alba

The "site:[website]" is the way you specify which website you want Google to return results from. In the example above, it is simply asking for results of anything that has "alba," from the LinkedIn website. After

---

11. http://google.com/support/websearch/bin/answer.py?hl=en&answer=134479&rd=1

the site:[website], you can put in whatever criteria you want. Glen's examples show some pretty sophisticated searches, narrowing down your results by LinkedIn Group, location, etc. X-ray searches are really quite powerful, although Glen's comparisons show that x-ray search results are not always necessarily complete.

In addition to using the search and advanced search tools, you should be able to find relevant contacts by participating in LinkedIn groups discussions, as well as browsing through the group members. Look for people with whom you share common interests and reach out to them. Don't overlook the Jobs section as a place to find decision makers at various companies.

Chapter Summary

- Finding people is a major reason most people are on LinkedIn. Don't expect everyone to find you—take the initiative to look for them through various channels.

- The quantity and quality of profiles you see in search results can be tied to the size of your network (and to how good your search criteria are).

- The advanced search form allows you to really narrow down your search, based on industry, job title, company, location, and more.

- Use Boolean and advanced search techniques to further narrow down the search results.

- Look for contacts and prospects in other parts of LinkedIn, such as groups, jobs, and the homepage.

"Take the time to look through the networks of your direct connects. This is where you can easily find people you'd like to connect with, and you'll know you can ask your contact to help with the connection."
Scott Ingram, CEO and Founder, Network In Austin

"Be sure to search the actual leadership competencies that matter, instead of keywords like job title and company name. Some of the best and most interesting thought leaders of the future I've met on LinkedIn are the ones who haven't worked at cookie-cutter company X doing cookie-cutter job Y. The team you assemble won't be filled with the limiting beliefs of your competitors from several years ago, which is a major plus."
David Dalka, Senior Marketing and Business Development Professional, http://www.daviddalka.com

7 Understanding Degrees of Separation

The basic idea behind "degrees of separation" is that you are only so many degrees away from anyone (historically, people have said we are six degrees away from anyone in the world). I've read that technology (LinkedIn, Facebook, and Twitter) has brought us much closer. Now they say we are only three or four degrees away from anyone we want to network with.

For example, if I want to meet the prime minister of some tiny country, I should be able to network into him or her by going to my second- and third-degree connections to get an introduction. That is, I talk to Mike (first degree) who says I should talk to Meagan (second degree) who says her friend Kim (third degree) knows the person and can make an introduction.

A few years ago there was a "Six Degrees of Kevin Bacon" experiment. Network television has done similar experiments to see if we really can meet someone by networking with them through our existing network. It might seem crazy, but you are probably just a few introductions away from talking to the person you've been trying to network with! The degrees-of-separation measurement LinkedIn uses gives you an interesting perspective on your network, although it can be misleading.

When you look at your network you can get a sense of the **breadth** (or width) and **depth** of your network. The width is depicted by the number of first-degree contacts in your network, and the depth is based on your contacts under your first-degree contacts.

Currently I have 7,534 contacts, which means that the first three degrees I have "reach" to almost 23 million people on LinkedIn. These seem like really big numbers, but it takes a lot of work to get value out of a first-degree network that big, and it's unthinkable that I might get value out of being "connected" to almost 23 million people.

In LinkedIn, you have certain privileges with your first-degree contacts that you don't have with other contacts. For example, I can see my first-degree contact's profile and contact information, but with many third-degree contacts I cannot see much. After LinkedIn became a public company, they started to restrict much of what I could see, so now I can see hardly anything from a third-degree contact's profile. If I want to contact them, I have to use an Introduction request instead of directly messaging them, like I can with a first-degree contact. Let's say I want to contact John Smith, a third-degree contact.

Instead of showing me John Smith's contact information, which I could see if we were first-degree contacts, LinkedIn shows me who I know who knows him, or, our mutual contacts. I would contact the person I'm connected with through a LinkedIn "introduction" that explains why I want to contact John, and an introductory note from me to John. My contact could then pass this introduction to his contact (which is my second-degree contact. I am then hopeful that he will send my request to John (my third-degree contact).

If each person really "knows and trusts" one another, it is more likely that they will pass the introduction on. Conceptually, this is a great idea, but there are two issues:

> **First,** there is no guarantee I have strong relationships with my connections. I personally haven't met many of my first-degree contacts. I might have some contacts who would not send on an Introduction request.

> **Second,** since the request travels through email, someone in the chain might not receive it in a timely manner. If it takes two days for each person to receive the email and forward it on, it might be six days before an Introduction request is even received by John! If you are in a hurry, it might be best to just pick up the phone.

I encourage you to look at your first-degree contacts' connections to see if there are people you should have a first-degree relationship with. You could invite them to connect with you. I mentioned that the degrees of separation could be misleading, and here's why: if I ask John to join my network, we lose the history of how we knew one another. John was once a third-degree contact, and I knew him because of the two contacts between us. I can see and track those relationships when he is a third-degree contact, but when we connect as first-degree contacts I lose the connection trail. I like to keep track of that trail, even if John and I have a better relationship than the two people between us. I think this creates a false idea of my network and my relationships.

The degrees-of-separation measurement is helpful as a data point, but it's only one (faulty) metric. I've seen people confuse the size, width, or depth of their network with the strength of their network. In addition to the size, think about, measure, or track the strength of the relationship with each person in your network. Keith Ferrazzi talks about this in *Never Eat Alone*. He emphasizes that networking is not just collecting names and numbers, but knowing how strong your relationships are. You can kind of track this in LinkedIn with notes or tags on each contact record, or you might consider tracking the strength of each relationship in your CRM.

Chapter Summary

- The "degrees of separation" concept gives you the ability to see how big your first-, second-, and third-degree networks are.

- The breadth and depth of your network doesn't necessarily indicate how strong your network is.

- When searching for new contacts, you can see the path between you and them.

8 Recommendations

LinkedIn recommendations are third-party pro-fessional endorsements. Don't confuse recommendations, which have been around for years, with the newer "endorsement" of skills. Endorsements are simply given with a click of a button, similar to "liking" someone's skill. It just adds one more like to their count, but there is no substance or authority behind an endorsement.

Recommendations carry weight because you cannot give one to yourself, nor can you edit a recommendation you've received. When you receive a recommendation, you can choose to show it on your profile or not, but you can't alter it. Only the person who wrote the recommendation can edit it. This gives more credibility to the recommendation.

To give a recommendation, find a contact you feel comfortable recommending and go to their profile page. You can start the recommendation process by clicking the down-arrow towards the top of their profile, or you can scroll down to the recommendation section and click the link to recommend them.

You have to say whether you are a colleague, service provider, business partner (which means neither of the previous two options), or had a student relationship (you were at the same school at the same time). I usually choose business partner since this is the closest descrip-tion for most of my contacts.

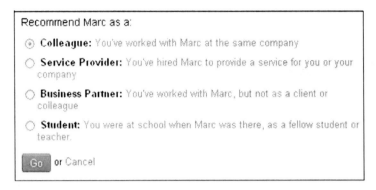

Figure 1: Recommend Contact

The next page asks me to clarify the relationship, where I choose my title and his title when we knew each other (or worked with one another). This is one of the clumsiest parts of the process for me because I've met many of my contacts through networking events, through volunteering, or because they've used JibberJobber or have read my blog. I choose the closest "right answer" so I can get to the actual recommendation.

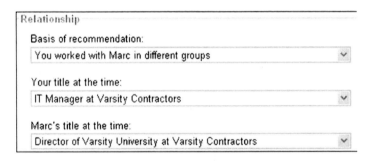

Figure 2: Clarify Relationship

The next box is where you write your recommendation. These are not long narratives. A recommendation is usually the length of a para-graph. Here's a recommendation I created for Marc, someone I used to work with and one of my first-degree contacts. Note that I left a blank line after the first sentence, but LinkedIn strips that out:

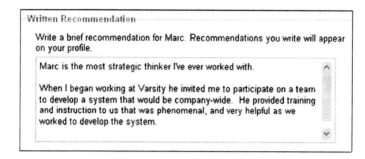

Figure 3: Written Recommendation

When I look at the quality of the recommendation, I'm looking for substance beyond the normal superficial cliché: "This person is awesome!" I want to know what specific value they bring to a product, team, company, or situation. The more evidence you provide in a recommendation, the strong your recommendation sounds. Reading a dozen "this person is great" recommendations gives me nothing, whereas reading a dozen recommendations where each person talked about the quantitative value the recommendee brings to the relationship, is really impressive.

After you write the recommendation and hit "Send," your contact will get an email with a link to display the recommendation. This will allow them to show it on their profile. Here is a snippet of the email I received after Janet gave me a recommendation:

> This recommendation is not yet displayed on your profile.
> **Display Janet Meiners - Janet@AffiliateFlash.com's
> recommendation**

Figure 4: Display Recommendation

When you click on the link, you are taken to LinkedIn, where you can choose to show or hide the recommendation. When I write a recommendation for someone it is not uncommon for them to ask for different wording. Such a request normally comes from people who are purposefully working on their brand. The most helpful requests suggest the wording that I should use to help exemplify their brand better. This process is similar to getting a letter of recommendation that isn't quite "right" and asking the person who wrote it to rewrite it, emphasizing different things.

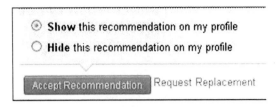

Figure 5: Show/Hide Recommendation

The best way to get recommendations is to ask people who you have worked with, or who admire your work, for recommendations. Another great way to get a recommendation is to recommend someone in your network. Since recommendations can be valuable endorsements used for business and personal branding and marketing, make sure you give the right message when you write them, and include specific details in the recommendations you give. The value of recommendations diminishes when they lack specific points.

TIP: If you want a recommendation, give a recommendation! You are more likely to get a good recommendation if you give one first.

It is okay to ask for specific wording in a LinkedIn Recommendation. When Janet was preparing my recommendation, she asked me if there was anything specific she should mention. This is an excellent time to communicate your brand to your contact, who might not understand the full scope of your current brand and offering. Take the opportunity to educate your contacts. This will make your recommendation more relevant to your current needs, and will give you a chance to reconnect with that contact in a meaningful and beneficial way.

As you work on getting the right recommendations for your own profile, consider these two points:

> **First,** some people think you can have too many recommenda-tions. I would never discourage someone from writing a recom-mendation for me. What's the right percentage of recommendations, based on the number of first-degree connec-tions? I don't have a specific answer, but when I'm asked that question I respond this way: I think you should have at least four to eight strong recommendations.

> **Second,** I have seen profiles of people who were in a job search and had a high percentage of recommendations from their previous company. When I see this, the recommendations from their

previous colleagues and executives seem faked. It's okay to have a lot of recommendations from previous colleagues, but try to get recommendations from other work or school experience.

Recommendations can be a powerful way to reach out to a contact and strengthen your relationship. I don't think you can really do this wrong, as long as you remember LinkedIn is a professional network, not the casual social networks that Facebook and Twitter are. Keep the tone of recommendations similar to what you would see in a letter of recommendation, and you will give your contacts a real gift they can use in their professional life.

Here are my top six suggestions regarding recommendations:

1. Only ask for recommendations from someone who can give you a real one.

2. Only give recommendations when you have something positive you can honestly say about the person.

3. Give recommendations without demanding one in return.

4. If you feel forced to give a recommendation, don't do it.

5. Give recommendations that are specific, speaking to professional competencies, skills, attributes, and characteristics.

6. Use pieces of recommendations in your marketing material, whether on your LinkedIn Profile (for example, in your summary) or your blog, business cards, etc.

Chapter Summary

- Adding recommendations to your profile is a great way to substantiate your strengths.

- Giving recommendations is an excellent way to reach out to your contacts and strengthen individual relationships.

- It is okay to ask for recommendations, just as you might ask for a letter of recommendation from a boss.

- It is okay to ask for revisions of a recommendation, especially if it isn't in sync with your branding strategy.

- Write recommendations that are specific and professionally endorsing, not vague or general.

- Use the recommendations in your other marketing tools.

"It's what you do and how you leverage your LinkedIn profile that makes you who you are to your network, and be memorable for time to come."
Dan Schawbel, Managing Partner, Millennial Branding LLC; Author, *Me 2.0***; and Publisher, Personal Branding Blog,** http://www.personalbrandingblog.com

"Meaningful recommendations from people you have worked with in a team or done projects for are the primary validation currency of positive attitude and achievements. It is the most important cutting edge tool for identification of these positive leadership traits. When hiring managers look at resumes, reading LinkedIn recommendations should always be the next tool used to narrow the pile."
David Dalka, Senior Marketing and Business Development Professional, http://www.daviddalka.com

9 Jobs

The Jobs section, LinkedIn's version of a job board, is one of the few features that survived the 2013 major design overhaul and stayed on the main menu. This is a big deal, considering the other features that were removed from the main menu, or were placed in a submenu.

A major benefit of LinkedIn's job board, which I haven't seen on any other job board, is that you can see who posted the job, what your relationship with that person is, and who your network contacts are in that company. Of course, you can also see how many degrees they are from you, how many recommendations they have (which might give you an indication of how effective reaching out to them through LinkedIn might be), and what their title is. I love seeing postings by a hiring manager, since that is exactly who I want to network into as a job seeker. If I'm doing competitive intelligence research, even as a salesperson, I just learned the name, title, and role of someone who is in a position of power.

TIP: Whether you are in a job search or not, use job boards to gather intelligence about your target companies and learn more about your industry.

Showing who posted the job sets LinkedIn apart from other job boards and is its most powerful feature. Can you imagine if every job board gave you information to help you network into the company with a path to network in, including names, contact information, and information that could help you drive the discussion? That's what LinkedIn is doing, and it is awesome!

Some people get excited at the idea that many jobs posted on LinkedIn are exclusive to LinkedIn users. I don't really care about that, or how easy it is to apply to a job. The real value of LinkedIn's job board is the networking information you can get on each posting.

In 2007, I did a search for jobs in New York City and got 415 results (job postings). In 2008, I did the same search and found 715 results. In late 2010, I did the same search and found 1,226 results. These results were based on a keyword search (in other words, I put "New York City" in the search box). A zip code search, using a New York City zip code (and a fifty mile radius) returned 2,662 results in 2010. The same search in 2014 returned 15,341 jobs.

A similar search on Indeed.com produced 135,763 jobs, almost ten times what LinkedIn is showing. A search on Linkup.com produced over 36,000 hits. I definitely wouldn't recommend LinkedIn as your main job board, but there are two reasons I would encourage you to use it:

> **First,** as mentioned, LinkedIn makes it easy to network into the job opening or company, with just a few clicks. Even as you use other job boards, you should cross-reference LinkedIn to see how you can network into target companies, and what you can learn about people who work there.

> **Second,** some opportunities are only posted on LinkedIn. Most job boards claim some kind of exclusivity of posted jobs, but because of what LinkedIn is, they have long attracted the HR community and recruiters who are looking for the best place to post jobs.

When I click on a job posting in LinkedIn, I can see how to network into the company. In addition to seeing who posted the job, and what their position is, I can see who can give me an introduction to that person. I can also see how many people are at that company, and in my network, which helps me figure out other ways to network into the company.

With tens of thousands of job boards available to job seekers and those doing competitive intelligence research, it is confusing to know which boards you should use. I suggest the LinkedIn job section as one to use because of the networking information you have access to.

Here are some ways you can get value out of LinkedIn's job postings:

1. **Do a salary search:** This is kind of a stretch because there isn't a salary or range search option, but you can try some figures to see what comes up. In the search box, I put in 100,000 and found a number of jobs that explicitly had 100,000 in the job description. To find the reference in the job posting, hold down Control+F and then type in 100 (this works on most browsers), which will show you each instance of 100 in the job description.

2. **Save relevant job postings:** It is easy to save a job posting, but why would you? Whether you are in a job search or not, job postings contain great information that you can use later. Let's say you apply to ten product manager jobs, but don't get a response from any of them. You then find out you are going to interview for a product manager role next week. One of the best places to go to prepare for the interview is to your saved jobs. Look at them, create word clouds, analyze the requirements and phrases used, and you will have great information to draw from as you prepare your interview responses. If you aren't in a job search, you can get a great idea of what your target companies are doing, where they are growing or hurting, and perhaps glimpse into their strategic direction.

3. **Map out the connections to your target companies:** Whether you create a rough organization chart (listing who works for who) with the information you can find on LinkedIn and their website, or list who used to work at that company, you should be able to get a nice overview of who you could talk to, about what, and what goals you would have from talking to different people.

Job boards are an excellent place to do research on a company. If your business has competitors or, you want to do research on a company's competitors, use job boards to see what's going on.

For example, let's say you are trying to figure out what direction a hiring company, or competitive company, is going. You search for them on any job board and find they have openings for two key roles in their customer service department. This might mean they are having significant customer service issues, or the role is impossible to keep staffed, which is something you heard about while talking to others. Or, it might mean they are expanding their customer base and they need more capacity in that department. If the same company is hiring ten sales executives in New England, and they haven't had a presence there before, you might guess they are expanding their efforts into New England. This could be critical competitive information!

Job boards may not have the best record for helping job seekers actually land a job. Statistics I read say only five percent to fourteen percent of jobs are filled because of job boards, and some say they are responsible for less than two percent! But without a doubt, job boards can be rich with competitive intelligence information! Use job boards, including the LinkedIn job board, to gather information about your target companies, figure out how to network with the right decision maker, and position yourself as a strong candidate or service provider!

Chapter Summary

- LinkedIn Jobs shows you the people in your network that have some tie to a posted job. This can help you network your way into a company.

- Use LinkedIn Jobs to do competitive intelligence research, whether you are looking for a job, looking for a customer, or just checking out your competition to understand the competitive landscape.

Chapter

10 Companies

When I wrote the first edition of this book, re-searching companies was limited to whatever you could find when doing a People Search. By the time I wrote the second edition, LinkedIn had made significant enhancements and added the companies section.

The addition of companies was significant. LinkedIn has a rich database of company infor-mation that is enhanced each time a user adds information to their own profile. LinkedIn shows some of this information to users. In the past, I would be able to see much more about a particular company. For example, I would be able to see where employees of my target company worked before they came to my target company, and then where they went after leaving said company. Unfortunately, this viewing option went away a while ago.

I can currently see affiliated companies, featured groups (usually the company's groups), and companies that other LinkedIn viewers looked at if they were interested in the same target company. This is powerful information, since I might not have known or thought of these tangential companies. This type of information expands my research.

Features of the company page have come and gone, but one thing I think will not go away is social commentary. That is, on the first page of a company page, you can see discussions and comments. As far as I can tell, this is initiated by the company page administrators or employees, but anyone can comment. This is a great place for them to put their news and highlight products, services, community involvement, awards, etc.

I can't start a discussion on a company page (like I can on a group), but I can comment on the discussions. If I were trying to network into a company, I would regularly check the new updates to see if there was something I could comment on. This would help me stay current on company happenings, and could help me put and keep my name and brand in front of people who need to see it.

I would also see who else is commenting on the updates to determine if I should network with them. For example, if my target company puts up an update, and someone who I think can be important as a networking contact comments on it, I would reach out to them and start a relationship.

When you click the "Companies" link under the Interests menu item, the simple search box changes to only search companies. You can also click on the Companies Home tab, which shows you the updates from companies you are following and a search box. You can search by industry, country, zip code (postal code), or by company name.

TIP: You should be able to list, right now, three of your target companies. What are they? Write them on this page, and then search for them on LinkedIn!

Another way to find a company page is from a user profile. Go to a profile of someone you want to network with, or someone who works at a company you want to network into. In their profile, wherever the company name is a hyperlink, you can click on it to go to the company page.

If you aren't sure what company you want to look at, or network into, think about the type of person you want to network with. I do this based on titles, roles, and location, and then I look at the companies listed on their profiles. Drilling down on those company profiles will then introduce new companies to me, and my research can go on and on.

You can easily add companies into LinkedIn's company database by clicking the "Add a Company" link, but you have to have a corporate email address. In other words, a Gmail address won't work unless you work at Gmail! You have to have a work address from that company.

I am regularly asked by small businesses and solopreneurs if they should have a company page. The assumption is that it is critical and great for

I'm on LinkedIn—Now What???

marketing. So far, I don't think it is important, and in some cases, a bad strategic move. People generally aren't going to LinkedIn (instead of Google) to look for information about your company. I think people going to company pages on LinkedIn are doing competitive and networking research, not making choices on buying products or services.

In my opinion, it's more important to have a great LinkedIn profile and your own company's website with the appropriate search engine optimization than to make a company page on LinkedIn. Even though it will not take much to create a company page, you aren't really providing value to customers and prospects. I don't think you are helping with an SEO strategy. The only thing you might be doing is sharing non-branded information that doesn't help attract customers or prospects. You might even make it easier for competitors to steal your key contractors or employees, and do deeper research about your company and strategy.

On the company page, you'll see a company summary at the top of the screen. This summary gives general information that you can find on Google or Yahoo! Finance. I would rather go to Yahoo! Finance to get this type of information as it is usually richer and more comprehensive. But they don't have comments and discussions there, like they do on LinkedIn.

As you would expect, you can figure out how to network into the company, as LinkedIn shows you how many first-, second-, and third-degree contacts you have at the company. If you are in sales, looking for partners, or if you are a job seeker trying to network into the company, you want to be sure to connect with people at the company. I've referred to this before as having relevant contacts. In this case, they are relevant to you because they are at one of your target companies. When I go to the Amazon company page, I see I have nine first-degree contacts and about 7,000 second-degree contacts. If I had fifty first-degree contacts at Amazon, I would certainly have many more second-degree contacts, which would really help me network into the company.

You can "follow" your target companies in LinkedIn. Once I follow a company I can choose when I want new updates and information about the company, and get those updates online or by email. You can choose to get updates when employees leave or join the company, or when they are promoted. You can get new job postings sent to you as well as any company profile updates. This would be a great way to keep news and opportunities from the company, but I honestly can't remember getting any company updates. Either it isn't working, or the updates go to my spam folders. This means you have to be more vigilant and go to the company page, instead of just waiting for an email to come to you.

Chapter Summary

- The company pages get data from various sources, which might provide you a rich tool for research.

- Use company pages to do competitive intelligence research on target companies, or competitors of your target companies.

- Find target companies by using the company search or by finding companies whose names are hyperlinked from profiles.

- Learn about your target company and determine how you could network your way into the company or strengthen your contacts in that company, based on who is already in your network.

"The Company Profile pages on LinkedIn are GOLD for anyone using LinkedIn to research companies, individuals, or positions within a company—and for recruiters searching for candidates! The Company Profile page contains a wealth of information on the company via Business Week and employment data compiled from the information current and former employees have entered in LinkedIn. This market intelligence is fantastic, allowing you to see hiring and promotional activity within the company, as well as quick links to additional information to research competitors, similar companies, etc. As a recruiter and avid networker, this is one of my favorite features within LinkedIn, and it can be used for business development and job search purposes in the same way."

Jennifer McClure, Executive Recruiter/Executive Coach; and President, Unbridled Talent, LLC,
http://unbridledtalent.com/blog

---

11 LinkedIn Groups

The value of LinkedIn groups has really increased since they took away LinkedIn answers. I used to say that answers was my #1 favorite feature in LinkedIn, and when LinkedIn added more functionality, I said it was a close second. Then they took answers away, and groups rose to be the very top of the list, as it is easily the most important feature. Once you have your profile set up, and when you choose to do a few proactive things on LinkedIn, groups need to be at the top of your list.

It is really easy to create a group, which means people have created many groups. You don't need to know about most of them—but there are a few you should know about! in the same way I encourage you to grow your network with relevant contacts, I want you to look for groups that are relevant to you. You can expand the concept of relevance from profession, geography, and industry to any area where you will find people who have like interests or needs.

There are many kinds of groups, including groups for alumni associations, professional affil-iations, industry interests, special interests, company alumni groups, and generational groups (GenY, GenX, Baby Boomers, etc.).

You can join up to fifty groups. I encourage you to find close to fifty and join them. Each group you join needs to be relevant to you. To join a group, simply click the join button on the group's page, or from the group's search results page. Some groups grant you membership automatically, while others have an approval process. For example, you can't join the Yale University Alumni group until they verify that you are an alumnus of Yale. If you are not automatically approved, you can send a message to the group administrator asking for approval to join I regularly get this type of "please let me join your group" requests from people who want to join my JibberJobber Career Management group (search "JibberJobber" in the groups directory to find my groups).

Once you become a group member you can browse through a list of members as well as search for people by keywords. Since each group you join will be relevant to you, most of the members should be, too. Take the time to look for key prospects you want to network with in your groups, and then reach out to them. Searching for people and making a list of who you find, is not networking. Make sure you initiate a conversation with them, and sometimes it will make sense to connect on LinkedIn. I say only sometimes because making a connection on LinkedIn isn't necessarily your primary goal. Your primary goal might be to create and nurture professional relationships, whether people connect with you or not.

One of the biggest benefits of joining a group is that you can message other group members, whether they are connected to you or not. The ability to message members is so powerful, I cannot overstate it enough. Usually if you want to communicate with someone through LinkedIn, you have to be a first-degree contact, or pay for an upgrade. Being a member of the same group treats your relationship with every other group member as if you were first-degree contacts. In other words, being members of the same group is a loophole to the upgrade. You can get the benefit of communicating with people who are not your first-degree contacts without having to pay. Until LinkedIn takes this feature away, I encourage you to use it!

Even if you don't do anything else with Groups, like search for members and comment on discussions, the ability to message members makes it worth it to find up to fifty relevant groups. Let me illustrate it this way: Imagine you only have five first-degree connections. You find a group relevant to you with one thousand members. You now have direct reach to each of the one thousand members of that group. It's as if you added one thousand people to your network. Multiple that reach by the fifty groups you can join and imagine the massive reach to relevant contacts you can have. There are plenty of groups that should be relevant to you that have more than a thousand people, and you should be able to join enough groups to allow you to access most of the people you ever need to access through LinkedIn. I'm in the Execunet group, with over 250,000 members, and the LinkedIn: HR group, with over 800,000 members. That is quite a reach!

I'm on LinkedIn—Now What???

In my business that I've been prospecting university career centers, I found five groups that career center professionals join and participate in, and I now have reach to thousands of career center professionals, without even connecting to them individually. When I find a profile of a career center professional I want to start a relationship with, I can usually communicate with them because they are a member of one of the groups I'm in. The alternatives to reaching out to people like this include (1) upgrading (2) or asking for an Introduction, neither of which I want to do, or (3) looking for their contact information on their profile, which I often cannot find.

Another significant feature in LinkedIn groups is what they call "discussions." Discussions gives you the ability to post a question or thought to the group, which all group members can see. You can also respond to questions or thoughts that other group members post. Group discussions present a significant opportunity to brand yourself as a thought leader and/or subject matter expert, *if you do it right.* There is plenty of spam and inappropriate content in group discussions. I encourage you to create conversations in the discussions so that others see value in them. Give valuable information and wise opinions that help others, and avoid bickering or preaching, or coming across as arrogant. You want people to see your name in their email or on the discussions page, and have them think, "Here is another comment from this person, I'm going to read it," instead of "Here is another comment from this person who always self-promotes and spams the group."

The ability to create discussions is almost like having a blog with a built-in audience. I say this because if you start blogging right now, you might have one person, or one hundred people, who read your posts. It is not easy to create an audience. If you go to a LinkedIn group, you could write something that might look like a short blog post and submit it to the group. Your reach is not a subset of the size of the group. As long as you are not self-promotional or spammy, you could have a great audience that is relevant to you very quickly. My advice is to respect the audience by posting information that is relevant to them, and making sure all of your communications are on-brand for you.

When you join a group, there are group settings you can adjust. One setting gives you the option to show the group logo on your profile. I can show my support for, and affinity toward, certain causes, associations, clubs, companies, and schools just by showing the logo on my profile.

You don't have to show all of your groups on your profile. Show only the groups that support the brand you've defined. Only show enough groups that get the point across. You can still have full membership in a group without showing the logo on your profile. You don't want to add more noise on your profile by showing too many groups.

Look for all of the relevant groups you can find and join them! Whether you have a proactive strategy and participate in group discussions, or you have a passive strategy and simply prepare to message other group members when you need to, you can't go wrong.

Owning Your Own Group

There are a lot of many groups, currently almost 1.9 million! Why would you start your own? There are quite a few good reasons. I started a group just so I could test out the features and see what it was like to be an owner. As a group owner, I can:

- approve new members, or remove people who spam the group or abuse their membership;

- moderate all discussions (not that I have to, but I can), and essentially have the last word; and

- send an "announcement," which is almost like a newsletter, to all group members.

To start your own group, go to the groups page and click on the "create a group" button. You'll need a name and description for your new group and, optionally, a logo.

Once your group is created, your job is to let people know about the group! There is no easy "tell everyone about my group" button. Let all of your network contacts, clients, and prospects know about the group through traditional methods. You can use your email signature, your website or blog, newsletters, comments you leave on other blogs, and group discussions to promote your new group. You can also use offline tools, such as business cards, to let people know about your group.

CAUTION: Be careful how you promote your group within similar groups. No one, especially the owner of other groups, wants to read messages that look like you are trying to steal group members.

When you create your group, make sure you have the right keywords in the description and summary, so people can find it when they search for a group like yours. What are the keywords that best describe your group? What are keywords your target audience would use to search for your group? List them out and then incorporate them into the group description. To get an idea of keywords you could use, visit competitive groups to see what they use.

One benefit of owning your own group is the viral marketing your personal and corporate brand can get. When group members put your logo on their profiles, they are advertising, and almost endorsing, you. Many of my JibberJobber Career Management members have the JibberJobber logo on their profile, which helps my branding.

Another way your group spreads virally is when someone joins the group, or contributes to a discussion. Their connections can see when they log in to LinkedIn, and their contacts' group activity. The viewer will see the title of the group discussion, and can click a link which takes them to your group, where they can see the discussion.

As the group administrator, don't be shy to develop your own rules and boundaries. When someone is abusing the group to send promotional messages, kick them out. Jump into the discussions when you have time, and keep the conversations alive. Take advantage of the announcements section, where you can send a message to each member's email box. This essentially turns your group into an opt-in newsletter, and I think it is the most powerful tool LinkedIn gives group owners. Don't abuse this feature, but if you neglect using it, I would suggest you are missing out on the main benefit of owning a group.

Let's wrap this chapter up. As a user of LinkedIn, I encourage you to:

- Seek out and join groups where your peers and target audience are. You can join up to fifty groups, but don't show all fifty group logos on your profile, as it will just clutter your profile. Join as many groups as you can.

- Go into your groups and browse the list of members. Use the group search box to find target prospects.

- Reach out to group members by sending direct messages through LinkedIn. Make sure you have a purpose to reach out to them and clearly communicate your purpose.

- Find discussions you can join or start. Pay attention to what you say, and how you say it, and avoid any netiquette missteps.

If you are interested in owning a group, I encourage you to:

- Go to Groups, click on the "Create a Group" tab, and get started on your own group!

- Market your group in as many places as you can. This includes your email signature, on blogs and websites, in comments you leave on other blogs, and in newsletters.

- Figure out how open your group is. If it's an alumni group, you'll want to limit access to alumni of the school or company. If it's a special interest group, you may need to be more open. Determine how open you'll be based on how much administration you want to do. For example, do you want to check out each applicant before you approve them? If not, make the group open.

- Spend time in your Groups Discussions to keep out spam and messages that would make the group less valuable to members. Encourage good conversations.

- Communicate to group members by initiating discussions and sending out announcements.

Participating in groups has added value to my LinkedIn experience. My group has around four thousand members. Other groups have hundreds of thousands of members. Don't discount smaller groups, since your voice might have a better chance of being heard by others and not get lost in the noise of a larger group. Big groups are great for the reach they give you, while smaller groups are great because you can have a bigger presence in a group with less discussions.

Can you see how groups could be an essential part of your LinkedIn strategy?

Chapter Summary

- Join groups where your peers or target audience are. Consider adding certain group logos to your profile.

- Communicate with other group members using groups discussions, and always keep it on-brand.

- Look for group members to see who should be in your first-degree network, and who you should initiate a relationship with.

- Consider starting your own group for your company, profession, industry, passion, and local geographic area.

"Administering a LinkedIn group is a terrific way to subtly raise awareness of yourself. It's a fairly simple process to start a group. Perhaps the most difficult part is designing your group's logo. I started and manage three groups, one for my high school and two for my geographic area, and I can see that most people who join them review my LinkedIn profile. That puts me in front of many people who may never have been aware of me otherwise. It also gives me the opportunity to welcome them and reach out to them as potential connections. It can work for you too, so consider what need is unfulfilled and start your own LinkedIn group."
Christine Pilch, Co-owner, Grow My Company; and Coauthor of *Understanding Brand Strategies: The Professional Service Firm's Guide to Growth*, http://www.growmyco.com

"Everyone knows that it's a good thing to network, but most people don't do it unless they need something. Building a LinkedIn network is a little like that. You really won't appreciate just how valuable your network has become until you need it. My advice is to start now! Take Jason's recommendations to heart and get going. When the time comes, you will be glad that you did."
Simon Meth, Corporate Recruiter & Career Counselor, Kettlehut and Meth, http://www.martinandsimon.com

Part III
Wrapping It Up

Part III discusses concepts for using LinkedIn in a personal branding strategy, warns you about shady practices that you might encounter, discusses netiquette, talks about complementary resources, and leaves you with some final thoughts.

12 LinkedIn for Personal Branding

I'm frequently asked how a company can make money with LinkedIn. Indeed, a company can and should, use LinkedIn for various reasons, including increasing sales.

In general, though, LinkedIn is a tool for individuals to network with individuals. The user profile is for one person, not for a company, product or service. I think your LinkedIn account should be yours, not your employer's. However, this is being debated in the courtroom, as recruiting firms and other companies claim building the network was done at work and is therefore owned by the employer.

Even though your LinkedIn profile is not a traditional corporate advertising channel, you can put language in your profile that explains what your company does in a way to attract new customers and evangelists.

Developing and sharing your personal brand is not as easy as filling out the fields in your profile. Understand what your personal brand currently is and then define what you want it to be. Some people think they don't have a brand because they haven't intentionally created it, and have a hard time defining it, but I would argue that everyone has a brand. It might not be what they want, but they have one. Figure out how you can strengthen what you want your brand to be, using online and offline tactics.

This is not a book on personal branding, so I won't cover all of the ins and outs of who you are or who you should be, nor explain all the ways you can share and reinforce your brand. I will, however, share some ideas on personal branding specific to LinkedIn. If you are interested in personal branding, I highly suggest the book *Career Distinction* by William Arruda and Kirsten Dixson. Another popular personal branding book is *Me 2.0* by Dan Schawbel, and his new bestseller, *Promote Yourself*. Two excellent, no-cost personal branding resources are Dan's popular Personal Branding Blog, http://www.personalbrandingblog.com, and the site "A Brand You World", http://www.personalbrandingevent.com, which has hours of recordings from its 2007 Global Telesummit that you can access for free.

Here are my recommendations for using LinkedIn to share and enhance your personal brand:

First, make sure you are showing the right information on your Public Profile. LinkedIn allows you to view your profile as others see it, but also log out to see what your profile looks like to people who are not logged in. People might find your profile from a Google search, or type your link in from a business card or resume when they are not logged in.

Is your profile showing enough information? Is it showing too much irrelevant information, and muddying your brand messaging)? Too many profiles show too little information, which forces me to spend time searching the Internet to find more information about you. Unfortunately, I don't have the time to do this, and I'm not going to assume the people who are looking for me will take the time. It there isn't enough information, I will move on to someone who has presented me with enough information to make a decision or pursue a relationship. Make it easy for people to learn about you without going to other websites.

Second, make your profile looks like you put work into it. Do everything you can from the profile chapter, and have the right stories and messaging to help people understand what your value-add and skills are. You can also take advantage of subtle branding opportunities, like changing your public profile URL from the default assigned value, which looks like gibberish, to something more descriptive of who you are. For example, my public profile ends in "/jasonalba" instead of something like "/1/234/698." If you see a link to my profile, you know exactly where you are going.

Changing your profile to a "vanity URL" is easy. I encourage you to change it to something like firstnamelastname, but you can put in something like ProductManagerWashington or something like that. I don't encourage you to change your vanity URL often (or ever).

Third, share the link to your LinkedIn profile. The easiest, most effective, and most viral way of sharing your URL is to put it in your email signature. Every time someone reads your email signature, they'll know how to easily learn more about you. Each time your emails get forwarded, more people will see your LinkedIn URL. Another way to share your profile is to put the "View My LinkedIn Profile" image on your personal website or blog.

NOTE: I DO NOT SHARE MY LINKEDIN URL LIKE THIS. Why not? I consider my LinkedIn profile a channel to get you to my other sites, which are where I want you to end up. If you don't have a website, blog, or other destination where you want people to end up, use your LinkedIn profile. But think about where you want people to end up and send them straight there, instead of through a channel.

I attended a presentation for job seekers about "regaining your personal identity," where the speaker talked about using resumes in networking events. He said that employed professionals don't hand out resumes, they hand out business cards. If you get a resume from someone, you have a preconceived idea about what they want, which is a job. There is an inherent message that you should help them in their journey to a new job. However, when someone gives you a business card, you are simply two peers, two professionals, exchanging contact information. There is no inherent message or obligation.

This concept applies to your LinkedIn profile. If you send a link with your resume in every email you send, you'll likely get into trouble with your employer. You'll send a message that you are in need of help, and the recipient might feel an unfair obligation. Sending a resume says, "I'm looking! If you can help, then let me know." However, sending a link to your LinkedIn profile says, "Here's my professional profile, check it out," which is a similar message that a business card gives.

Your LinkedIn profile will have much of the same information found on your resume, with matching quantifying statements. Sending someone to your profile will help them understand your accomplishments and experience without implying any obligation.

Finally, if you leave a comment on a blog, online news article, forum, or some other website, you have two opportunities to leave a link to your website. If you don't have your own website or blog, enter the link to your LinkedIn profile. The first place to put a URL is in the "website" box.

The second place to leave a URL is at the end of your comment, much like what you would do in an email signature. Make it easy for the reader to click a link to learn more about you!

Chapter Summary

- Use LinkedIn to strengthen your personal brand.

- Your LinkedIn profile is kind of like a resume, without many of the limitations (length) and negative connotations ("I'm a job seeker, help me!") that a resume might have.

- Use your Public profile URL as your website address when you comment on blogs, unless you have a blog or other website you would prefer people go to. Know which sites are your channels and which sites are your destinations.

13 Shady Practices

With as many users as LinkedIn has, you are almost guaranteed to run into people who don't abide by common netiquette or the LinkedIn User Agreement. You can see the User Agreement by scrolling to the bottom of some pages on LinkedIn. Right now they have a glitch on self-refreshing pages, like the home page and company pages, so even if I scroll to the bottom it gets bumped down. The easiest way to see the User Agreement, or any footer link, is to go to a page that doesn't self-refresh, like your own profile.

Over the years, I've seen a number of violations of common sense and good networking. I'm sure that if you have read this far, you have no intention of acting shady on LinkedIn. Here are some actual practices I've seen that are considered to be questionable:

Email in name field. This is a very simple, almost non-offensive deed, but I mention it because it is against the terms set forth in the LinkedIn User "Dos" and Don'ts" section of the User Agreement[12], and LinkedIn has suspended accounts for non-compliance. In the User Agreement, it says that the user agrees not to post "to a content field content that is not intended for such field." For example, putting an email address or even a phone number in a name or title field. This may be the most common offense, to the point where it looks like "everyone is doing it." Maybe everyone is doing it, but it is still against the rules, and you might get penalized.

---

12. http://linkedin.com/static?key=user_agreement

Tollboothing. This is when people charge you to have access to their LinkedIn connections. As I mentioned, you can do a search and find people in their network, but if you want an introduction or some kind of endorsed communication with one of their contacts, they will charge you money. The logic behind this is that they have put a lot of time and effort into building their network, networking is a big part of their livelihood, and that you should expect to have to pay for their "services." I don't agree with this behavior, and most people are surprised or shocked when they get a response from a tollbooth person. If I meet someone who wants me to pay for a connection, I disconnect from them because it is so contrary to the spirit of networking. Doing something like this might hinder your networking and LinkedIn strategy.

Lying. One of the best ways to be found by companies that hire Yale graduates is to put that you graduated from Yale. You can easily put Yale as one of the schools you went to. You can easily lie about places that you worked and where you went to school. You can actually lie about anything on your profile, which is one reason why recommendations carry so much weight. Some people put false information on their LinkedIn profile to increase their chances of being found by recruiters or hiring managers, or to make a stronger impression. Don't do this.

Vincent Wright, networking enthusiast and Chief Branding Officer of Brandergy, found a profile where the person had supposedly worked for fifteen years in one hundred different companies. Vincent called him the 1,500-year-old man (100 companies x 15 years at each company = 1,500 years of work experience!). Vincent was a professional recruiter, and professional recruiters can see deception from a mile away. Make sure your profile is clean and verifiable, just as your resume should be.

What should you do if someone contacts you because of a commonality with a school or company listed on your account? On an email listserv, Scott Allen recommended the following:

> If someone sends you an invitation saying they're a former colleague or classmate, at least take a look at the dates and other entries on their profile and make sure they jibe. If they don't have a full position and description listed, that's a yellow flag.

It's up to you to make sure the person you connect with, or respond to, is who he says he is. I wouldn't expect LinkedIn to verify information on their profile. When I get a communication from someone on LinkedIn that is blatantly fraudulent, I forward the message to the customer support email address with hopes their account gets deleted. We don't need more spammers on LinkedIn.

I'm on LinkedIn—Now What???

Using LinkedIn groups to cloak inappropriate promotion. The LinkedIn community has been clear they don't want groups to turn into a spam-laden area, generating useless requests for information adding more noise to people's inboxes. If you post a few discussions (or comments on discussions) that are borderline spam, you'll probably have some people respond about it being inappropriate. Abusing your membership in a group will not only add clutter to the group and diminish the value of its discussions, but will also show you don't respect group members. You don't want to be that person whom everyone thinks is a spammer.

Fishing for fake recommendations. You can't make up recommendations for your profile, and creating fake profiles to endorse your main profile is too much work for most people. Some people ask for recommendations without knowing you. The shady part is when someone you don't really know, or haven't worked with, asks for a recommendation. It usually comes like this: "If you recommend me, I'll recommend you." I used to respond with something like this: "I don't really feel like I know you well enough to give you a recommendation—sorry. I'd like to get to know you better before I write a recommendation." I have never gotten a response back, and now I don't even bother sending that message. I think some people send requests for recommendations to their entire network without realizing it, so I just ignore them.

Fishing for email addresses. Because so many people violate the rule about not putting email addresses in the name field, it's easy to find email addresses to add to your mailing list. I'm not suggesting that you collect them to put on your newsletter or mailing list, but here's how easy it is. Just search ".com" in the search box (start with the last name field), and you'll find plenty of email addresses to add to your list. It's that easy to find email addresses to spam!

These are not all of the shady practices, but I share these with you because I want you to know that no everyone on LinkedIn has honest intentions. The key is to be cautious with the information you find, and be careful with the information you give.

Chapter Summary

- People will do things wrong, sometimes even unknowingly. Beware of whom you interact with, and how you interact with them. If they accidentally do something wrong, forgive them and move on in the relationship.

- If you violate LinkedIn policy, you risk having your account suspended, or being seen as someone that does not respect "the rules."

On Netiquette

There are plenty of opportunities to make etiquette mistakes with your contacts on LinkedIn and other social sites. Netiquette refers to etiquette, or acceptable social behavior, online (hence, the "net").

It's critical to understand some basic rules of Internet etiquette. Not understanding can have consequences as simple as people ignoring you, and as complex as getting kicked out of various forums and websites, or even getting blacklisted by industry influencers. In addition to having an online presence and developing your personal brand, you should stay within the boundaries of your professional brand. Let me assume some component of your brand is awareness, professional consideration, and respect. Even if people consider you to be aggressive, you should still have respect for the rules of interaction. Here are some basics rules to consider:

1. **Be nice. Be concise.** Always be concise! Aren't we in the habit of *skimming* more than reading? We are faced with massive amount of information from all sides: email, social websites, Internet searches, blogs, news sites - the list doesn't seem to have an end! Write concise messages, with a nice tone, and you'll have your message read and responded to more often. Write a long message and I'll save it for later, when I'm not busy. Can you guess when that will be? Probably never.

2. **Avoid sarcasm in your online communications.** We should be very careful with funny "jokes" and sarcasm in the written word. I frequently hit the backspace button when writing many of my emails because something that sounded good while I wrote it could be interpreted in the wrong way. Furthermore, jokes or sarcasm can be a distraction from my real message, when I want to make my intentions clear.

3. **Assume people have good intentions.** Scott Allen advises people to "presume good intent" when reading an email that might come across as negative, harsh, or inappropriate. Scott is right! You know you should be careful when sending messages, but some of your contacts might not have gotten the memo on netiquette. Give them the benefit of the doubt, and reread their message assuming they wrote it with good intentions.

4. **Don't chastise or preach.** I've seen too many online discussions go from bad to worse when one person chastises or preaches their opinion. They try to advocate the only right way to do, or think about, something. What starts off as a general admonition or knowledge-sharing email can easily turn into personal jabs and accusations. I've found it is much more effective to just bow out of the discussion and move on to something else, even if you don't get the last word. Everyone involved will appreciate the thread dying down, and you'll look more mature, wiser, or just smarter for not pursuing an online fistfight.

5. **Consider cultural differences when reading or writing anything.** Many groups I'm in have a good representation of people from all walks of life, and from different countries. There are people whose native tongue is not the same as everyone else on the list. There are people who are right out of school, or still students, and others who are at the end of their career. There are entrepreneurs, executives, artists, rich people, and poor folks. These differences affect the messages and even the culture of the online forum, and can lead to misunderstandings.

6. **Know when to take it off-list.** Lots of topics discussed online are interesting and appropriate. However, sometimes they are only interesting and appropriate to the two people participating in the discussion. If this is the case, take the discussion off-list. Taking a discussion off-list means to continue the discussion outside of the general group. If the discussion starts off slightly off-topic and it gets deeper and more technical, take it off-list. If the discussion is between you and only one other person, or a small subset of the group, and does not add value to anyone else, take it off-list. If the discussion is completely off-topic for the group, or personal, take it off-list. Even if you are just saying "thank you," or "happy birthday" or something like that, do it off-list.

I'm on LinkedIn—Now What???

There are always exceptions to the rules. Remember this: everything you write, whether it's a comment, an email, an instant message, or anything, may come back to haunt you. I like the rule of thumb, even the caution, to write everything as if it will be printed on the front page of a major newspaper, with full credit back to me!

Chapter Summary

- Learning the rules of netiquette will help you maintain the proper relationships as you communicate with people online.

- Understanding netiquette mistakes may help you be more understanding or patient with people who don't understand them.

15 Complementary Tools and Resources

I have grown to love and appreciate real networking. I've loved destroying my assumptions of what networking was, including simply collecting names and numbers, passing out as many business cards as I could, and collecting business cards. I've enjoyed focusing more on developing and nurturing real relationships. LinkedIn has been an important, valuable part of my networking strategy. There are other network tools I recommend that complement LinkedIn. This chapter lists those tools.

In addition to networking and relationships, many people use LinkedIn as a part of their online personal branding strategy. They develop a profile much like they would develop a resume, trying to optimize it so people will

a. find it when searching for keywords (such as "project manager"), and/or

b. be interested in working with, hiring, or learning more about the person.

If you are interested in developing an online presence, there are other ways to do it. A public profile on LinkedIn should only be one part of your multi-faceted strategy. Here's a short list of ways to enhance your online presence, and even get your name on the front page of search engine results:

- Find other sites that allow you to have a public profile, such as JobSpice.com and VisualCV.com. There are easily dozens of sites that allow you to have a profile that search engines can access. However, the list of websites changes regularly as companies go out of business. The previous edition of this book had three other websites that I had to remove. Don't spend too much time on other sites that might not be around next year.

- Set up a blog that allows you to brand yourself and quantify your professional **breadth** and **depth** in a very powerful way.

- Consider a Twitter account. I have used it for many years and honestly, I've fallen out of love with it. But some people are still finding value in Twitter.

- Comment on other blogs to establish your online presence and footprint, pointing back to a central place. This central place can be your blog or one of your online profiles, like your LinkedIn Public Profile.

- Develop a Squidoo lens where you can list things such as your online profiles, favorite books, and blog feeds. The goal is to help people understand your professional interests and abilities and to be found when people search for certain keywords.

- Write articles and post them for free online (search for article directory, or ezines, to see where you can easily post articles online), or volunteer to write a column for a magazine or newspaper.

All of these tools and tactics complement one another. On your LinkedIn profile, list your other websites, profiles, and articles. On your blog, list your LinkedIn profile and links to your articles and other online activity. This allows someone who finds one of your profiles to visit your other pages where they might learn more about you.

Having a presence on many different platforms might help you connect with others in a place where they feel comfortable. For example, your target audience might be on Twitter or Facebook, but not on other sites. Or maybe they aren't on any of the social sites, and they will most likely only find you when they use a search engine. Having multiple profiles can help search engines find you.

In addition to social tools and online profiles, use a CRM. There are hundreds of relationship management tools available to help manage your relationships. Recruiters use a relationship tool to track their job candidates, which they call an applicant tracking system. They make notes on candidates, and create log entries and action items to help them as they try to fill job openings. Salespeople have customer relationship management tools. They use these to help manage information about prospects and clients. Why shouldn't you have something to help you manage your own relationships, especially if you are serious about being CEO of Me, Inc.?

I'm a strong advocate of using a relationship management tool. In 2006, shortly after I got laid off, I realized my networking efforts were significantly lacking. To help other job seekers and professionals who might be in a transition, I designed a system for the average person who had no experience in sales. JibberJobber.com has become my relationship management tool, and has helped many people network better.

The relationship management tool you use could be as rudimentary as an Excel spreadsheet (good luck with that), as complex as a salesperson's contact relationship management suite (which might require weeks of training and customization to use), or as simple and common as Microsoft Outlook's Contacts section (which can be good enough for very small networks and no follow-up, but lacks important CRM features).

Industrial-level tools, such as the salesperson's ACT!, GoldMine®, or Salesforce.com, are quite common. JibberJobber.com was designed to manage your personal relationships in a career management context. Anyone interested in climbing the ladder, creating "job security," or developing and nurturing a professional network would find JibberJobber.com useful. No matter what you choose, use something in addition to LinkedIn.

Other social networking sites have made considerable progress as they offer professional networking opportunities. Twitter and Facebook are regarded as tools where professionals can network, but Facebook lacks degrees of separation, as well as a strong search interface. If they were to add or enhance those two features, they would present a considerable threat to what LinkedIn offers. Twitter can be powerful, but it has a very simple feature set and lacks a lot of features that LinkedIn offers.

I don't advocate the use of one social network over another since they might be perfect complements. When I consider using a new networking tool, I ask a few questions. Will this tool help me:

- Expand my network within my country?

- Expand my network internationally?

- Voice my opinion and develop my personal brand with a targeted audience?

- Learn from other like-minded professionals?

There are many resources to keep up with what's going on at LinkedIn. LinkedIn's own blog and learning center have matured significantly and can provide you with information on new features. Here are some other resources:

- My **ImOnLinkedInNowWhat.com** blog—I started this blog to serve as a supplement to this book. It has become a great resource where I can flesh out ideas from the book, talk about current issues, and respond to readers' questions. There are many years of blog posts here.

- The **Linked Intelligence** blog[13]—Scott Allen's blog which has some great posts explaining techniques and strategies to help us understand how we can get more value out of LinkedIn.

- The **LinkedIn User Agreement** page[14]—If you are serious about using LinkedIn, you should read this at least once. Don't worry, it is short and fairly easy to read. There are a number of violations that might cause LinkedIn to freeze your account. Get familiar with the rules and philosophies behind the rules and you should be okay.

- The official **LinkedIn Blog**[15]—This blog has excellent information and news for LinkedIn users and fans, and it's directly from LinkedIn. There are many authors on this blog so you get a good mix of information, including recent feature updates, LinkedIn best practices, etc.

- The **LinkedIn Users Manual** blog[16]—Peter Nguyen has good ideas on making money with LinkedIn, selling knowledge, etc. I don't subscribe to any "get rich quick" methodology and haven't followed his stuff that much, but he has some great ideas, even if he doesn't post frequently

- Deb Dib's article, "**LinkedIn—What It Is and Why You Need to Be On It**"[17]—This is an excellent article written for executives in career transition. There are eight links to very compelling LinkedIn profiles that you must check out as you optimize your own profile.

- The *LinkedIn Personal Trainer* is a book by Steve Tylock. I wish I could say I wrote the first book on LinkedIn, but Steve got his

---

13. http://www.linkedintelligence.com
14. http://linkedin.com/static?key=user_agreement&trk=ftr_useragre
15. http://blog.linkedin.com
16. http://linkedinusermanual.blogspot.com
17. http://job-hunt.org/executive-job-search/linkedin-for-executives.shtml

book out shortly before the first edition of mine came out. Steve's book has worksheets you can use as to help get your LinkedIn strategy up and running. You can find more information at http://www.linkedInpersonaltrainer.com.

In addition to these resources, do not underestimate a solid networking book to learn some networking basics. Online networking and offline networking have many things in common, the greatest of which is that networking is all about relationships. Here are some great networking books I recommend:

- *Never Eat Alone*[18] by Keith Ferrazzi—I read this book when I thought networking was all about desperate people schmoozing and passing business cards for self-gain. Keith changed my perspective on what networking is and how to do it. I strongly, strongly recommend this book to anyone who asks about networking.

- *Some Assembly Required* and *The ABC's of Networking* by Thom Singer[19]—Thom's books are great resources with hundreds of practical, right-now relationship building tips. I've found his writings to be especially applicable in the corporate environment, because he gives many examples on how to enrich customer and prospect relationships.

- *Dig Your Well Before You're Thirsty*[20] by Harvey Mackay—This has been a staple of networking books for many years. Harvey Mackay has written a number of best-seller books on networking and career management, and is an authority in this space.

- Jeffrey Gitomer's *Little Black Book of Connections: 6.5 Assets for Networking Your Way to RICH Relationships*[21]—I got this book as a gift from a friend, and it's a gift I cherish. I've been asked by multiple people to include this book as a recommendation.

Use the Google Blogs search at http://blogsearch.google.com to see current buzz about LinkedIn from bloggers. I've listed some of my favorite resources, but I'm sure there are other helpful gems I haven't come across yet.

---

18. http://www.keithferrazzi.com
19. http://thomsinger.com/
20. http://harveymackay.com
21. http://gitomer.com

Chapter Summary

- Tools to complement LinkedIn include CRM software, discussion forums, and other online profile, networking, and social websites.

- Resources to complement this book include blogs, websites, and other books.

- LinkedIn should be only one facet of your online social strategy.

- Subscribe to **ImOnLinkedInNowWhat.com** to keep current on LinkedIn issues, news, thoughts, and techniques.

16 Conclusion

You should now have a good grasp on how to get the most out of LinkedIn from a "how to" angle, as well as a "why should this matter to me" angle.

Here are some parting thoughts:

- Know what you want to get out of LinkedIn (and related technologies), and make a strategic plan to accomplish that.

- LinkedIn continually changes their product and features, thus continually changing your experience and the value you get. Focus on your goals and objectives, and use LinkedIn as a tool, but realize the features you like right now might change tomorrow.

- Use LinkedIn as the tool that it is and find complementary tools to fill the gaps.

- Explore the premium upgrade options, toolbar plugins, and other things from LinkedIn to get more value out of it.

- Create a strategy to enhance your personal brand and make sure the tools and tactics you use will help you execute that strategy.

- Think about career management whether you are employed or not, happy or unhappy, a business owner or an executive. Think about how all of these tools can help you execute your career management strategy.

- Realize your entire network is not in LinkedIn. Don't neglect the rich networking opportunities outside of LinkedIn.

Do you have thoughts or ideas for the next edition of this book? Please email me: Jason@JibberJobber.com.

- Sign up to follow new and current topics at **ImOnLinkedInNowWhat.com**.

- If you found this book valuable, please leave a review on Amazon.com. Simply search for LinkedIn Now What on Amazon's home page.

LinkedIn is a great tool—but just like the power tool in your garage, it's useless until you learn how it works, and then actually put it to use!

Good luck!

"Take your connections offline. LinkedIn is a great tool, but don't forget that other tools still exist. Your phone still works, and there's nothing better than a face-to-face connection."
Scott Ingram, CEO and Founder, Network In Austin

"LinkedIn doesn't replace traditional networking; it facilitates it. Always supplement your online efforts with face-to-face networking."
Barbara Safani, Owner, Career Solvers,
http://www.careersolvers.com

"LinkedIn is a great tool, but you need to learn to use it and you have to maintain it to keep it sharp! Take the time to investigate all the features, encourage colleagues and friends to not only join your network but build their own so you can leverage each other's contacts, and schedule LinkedIn activities with yourself—like updating your profile once a month."
Deb Dib, The CEO Coach,
http://www.executivepowerbrand.com

Appendix

A LinkedIn for Job Seekers

How can job seekers use LinkedIn in their job search? The same way a salesperson uses LinkedIn: finding new contacts, doing research on them, contacting them, and doing company research. Here are specific ways a job seeker can use LinkedIn:

1. **Fix your profile.** Your profile should NOT communicate, "Please hire me, I'm desperate!" It should say "I'm a professional and I bring value to my employer, customers, contacts and industry." Make sure your profile is pristine, with NO typos, no grammar issues, and no noise. Craft your summary and every word in your profile so you come across as professional. Remember, you are a professional in transition, not a "professional job seeker."

2. **Search for your target companies.** You should have at least five target companies you are focusing on. These are the companies you really want to work for. Search for them and find out who in your network has ever worked there, as well as what key employees you can network with.

3. **Grow your network strategically.** Find people who have contacts in your target companies and invite them to connect. Work on developing a real relationship with them. Invite them to lunch, ask for informational interviews, or call them on the phone to get more information about opportunities and other people you should contact. As you add

contacts from your target companies to your LinkedIn network, you'll get better results in your searches.

4. **Browse through your key contacts' contacts to look for professional or industry leaders with which to connect.** Ask for an introduction to contacts, and try to start a relationship with these leaders. Continue to network deeper, asking yourself, "Who do you know?"

5. **Use the advanced search page.** Search for contacts with the job titles you are applying to. Search for contacts who work, or have ever worked, at your target companies. Search for contacts that have key titles in industries you are interested in, and for contacts who are in certain geographic areas. Find these contacts and work on communicating with each of them. Look for people who can give you information you need to have a successful job search.

6. **Ask questions regularly.** Use the status update on the homepage and group discussions to ask questions. These questions should help establish your brand with your network and people who are relevant to you. Don't ask questions that can be interpreted as "I need a job, please help me!" Instead, ask questions that develop you as a subject matter expert and/or thought leader. As your network learns more about you, and what you do (or want to do), they'll be more prepared to help you.

7. **Participate in the right group discussions.** When you participate in group discussions you get to communicate your brand with *other people's networks*. Your contributions MUST be value-add, informational, or on-brand. As you participate in group discussions, you might get invitations to connect with people who probably have something in common with you.

8. **Ask for introductions.** When you find someone you want to network your way into, or connect with on LinkedIn, use the introductions feature. You will help your first-degree contacts understand what kind of contact you want to talk with, AND what your branded message is to them. Make sure you write your introduction requests concisely, and with a compelling message, so both parties can learn more about you.

9. **Browse the network updates on the homepage to see who you can reach out to.** You are probably connected with dozens, hundreds, or thousands of people who are relevant to you. Communicate with them! Too many times I see people not communicating with their LinkedIn contacts, and they miss rich opportunities to nurture relationships, communicate their brand, and be in the right place at the right time.

10. **Use the job search tool to find out who else to network with.** The real value of the jobs section is that you can see who you know in companies that have open opportunities, and network with them. Always work to network into an open job.

11. **Find groups to join.** Look for groups that would have people in your profession, industry, target companies, or even city or state. Joining groups that are relevant to you should significantly increase the value you get out of Groups, as long as you actively participate in them.

12. **BONUS IDEA: Share your LinkedIn knowledge and experience with others at job clubs and networking groups.** Become "that person" who shares tactics and techniques with other job seekers, especially those who have the deer-in-the-headlights look. They will be forever grateful to you for sharing your knowledge, and you'll set yourself apart as a giver. As you teach others, you'll learn more about LinkedIn.

B LinkedIn for Sales Professionals

Sales professionals can use LinkedIn to grow their networks, learn about prospects, perform research for sales opportunities, and communicate with decision makers. Here are specific ideas for sales professionals to get more value out of LinkedIn:

1. **If your profile isn't complete, I might not trust who you are when you reach out to me.** Flesh out your profile with relevant information to help me learn about you, and maybe even get to a point where I trust you. Your profile should have a lot of "what's in it for me" language to your prospect, as opposed to bragging to industry colleagues about how great you are at sales.

2. **Search is your friend.** List the keywords your target segment would have in their profile, including position, role, company, industry, interests, and associations. Go into the advanced people search page, and do searches using advanced search strings.

3. **Grow your network shamelessly.** Okay, I mean that tongue-in-cheek, as I wouldn't tell you to blindly add people to your network. But if you want to use LinkedIn for sales, it might make sense to have a large network and be an open networking strategy. I'm not talking hundreds of first-degree contacts; I'm talking thousands.

4. **Grow your network strategically.** Do you sell stuff in one indus-try? You should amass contacts from that industry. Don't worry about the person's job title. A receptionist in your

target industry might have excellent contacts, and considerable power. Target contacts from adjacent industries. Those contacts should have contacts in your target industry. Your growth strategy could also include specific types of professionals (accountants and CFOs, for example) or people in a certain geography, if your target audience is geographically based.

5. **Ask for introductions from your connections.** When you find someone you want to communicate with, use LinkedIn introductions to ask your first-degree contacts for a warm introduction. This will put your branded message in front of your first-degree contacts again. This gives you a chance to strengthen your relationship with them. Nurture individual relationships so you don't just take, take, take in the relationship.

6. **Fill in downtime when you are on the road.** Do a mile radius search to look for contacts where you'll be. Use keywords to narrow the search results down to the right people. Consider hosting a LinkedIn get-together and inviting as many LinkedIn contacts as you can for dinner. Search the right groups to see if there are active local groups to promote the dinner.

7. **Have discussions in groups with your target audience (not your peers).** As your prospects read your discussions and comments they will likely know you are in sales, so don't try to hide that. Be genuine. Ask questions they can answer, and questions that they would want to know the answers to. You want to be known as a thought leader, and/or a subject matter expert. You also want to become a connector for them. Regular participation in group discussions should help increase brand awareness for you and your company.

8. **Comment on discussions in groups where your prospects are.** Think about how others will perceive you based on your responses. Be comprehensive, kind, and share your with expertise. Share information and recommend other experts, including your customers and prospects (if appropriate).

9. **Join groups where your audience is and where their contacts are.** In addition to participating in group discussions, browse through the group members to look for prospects. Send group members messages with clear, concise language to focus on your long-term, professional relationship, but also let them know why you want to connect.

10. **Consider advertising on LinkedIn.** LinkedIn advertising gives you the ability to show different ads to different LinkedIn users. It's comparatively expensive, but the ads go in front of a demographic that is supposedly above average in regard to income, professional status, and decision-making power. There is a $10/day minimum spending fee, so this will cost at least $300/month if you have the ad on every day.

About the Author

Jason Alba is *the* job seeker and networking advocate. He got laid off in January 2006, just a few weeks after Christmas. Even though he had great credentials and it was a job-seeker's market, Jason could hardly get a job interview. He decided to take a step back and figure out what the job search process was all about. Within a few months, he designed the personal job search tool, JibberJobber.com, which helps professionals manage career and job search activities the same way a salesperson manages prospects and customer data with a CRM.

Jason is a highly regarded speaker, sharing career management and social marketing messages with thousands of professionals each year, from California to Istanbul. Learn more at **JasonAlba.com**.

Other Happy About Books

Storytelling About Your Brand Online & Offline

Bernadette Martin demonstrates how stories have transformed corporate images as well as professionals' careers.

Paperback: $22.95
eBook: $16.95

I'm on Facebook—Now What??? (2nd Edition)

This book explains the different parts of Facebook and helps you understand how you can get the most out of your Facebook account.

Paperback: $19.95
eBook: $14.95

Social Media Success!

This book is a launch pad for successful social media engagement. It shows how to identify the right networks, find the influencers, the people you want to talk to and which tools will work the best for you.

Paperback: $19.95
eBook: $14.95

I'm at a Networking Event—Now What???

Through this book you will learn how to make quality connections, cultivate relationships, expand your circle of influence through networking events, and create good "social capital."

Paperback: $19.95
eBook: $14.95

Purchase these books at Happy About
http://happyabout.com
or at other online and physical bookstores.

More Praise for *I'm on LinkedIn—Now What???*

"If you're confused, frustrated, or overwhelmed by LinkedIn and wondering how to reap the benefits others have, you need the information in this book."
Winnie Anderson, Chief Strategy Maven, Client Focused Marketing,
http://clientfocusedmarketing.com/

"Whether for job search or for making business connections, Jason Alba's book offers a logical, common sense approach to using LinkedIn. He cuts through the clutter by providing simple, concise, and remarkably well-communicated strategies for using this tool efficiently and effectively.

Far from overwhelming the reader with pages of stepwise instructions and screen prints, Jason instead shares his journey with learning and using the tool, while offering still more value with additional tips and suggestions, as well as insight from other users.

I'm on LinkedIn—Now What??? offers a quick, easy, and effective way to learn, understand, and execute a solid online strategy. It provides mindset and foundation—two important aspects to help one build more visibility and credibility. While I've used LinkedIn for years, I still found value in every chapter. A great business book and reference—and an enjoyable read—it has my complete endorsement."
Tara Kachaturoff, Producer and Host, Michigan Entrepreneur TV,
http://www.michiganentrepreneurtv.com

"Whether you are looking to advance your career or build a business, LinkedIn can be, and should be, an important part of your strategy. In I'm on LinkedIn— Now What???, Jason Alba helps you understand how to get the most out of LinkedIn. Whether you are a LinkedIn novice or a seasoned veteran, you will find information to help take your LinkedIn experience to the next level. LinkedIn is a powerful source for job leads, career advice, sales leads, receiving invitations for speaking engagements, and more. Why search for your next position when the next opportunity can find you? I'm on LinkedIn—Now What??? will help people with the right opportunities to find you."
Larry Boyer, Director of Decision Analytics, IHS, http://www.ihs.com/**; and President, Success Rockets,** http://www.successrockets.com/

"In my work as a career counselor and resume writer, Jason Alba helped me to integrate the massive confusion about how to utilize LinkedIn—as a job search tool for my clients and as a solopreneur to promote my business. There is no option for failing to learn LinkedIn if you buy this social media book."
Mindy Thomas, Founder and Principal, Thomas Career Consulting,
http://www.thomascareerconsulting.com

"Leveraging LinkedIn for your professional success takes more than publishing your professional profile and hoping someone will contact you about that next career or business opportunity. You really need to invest in learning how to get the most out of your membership. I'm on LinkedIn—Now What??? is a guidebook that will help you fast-track your success by navigating the powerful features of the platform whether you are at the start of your career or a seasoned professional."

Krishna De, Online Visibility Expert, Social Media Speaker, and Mentor, http://krishnade.com

"Even though I'm a professional resume writer, I was turning down clients' requests to assist them with their LinkedIn profiles. I said I was too busy, but the truth was I was too embarrassed to admit I didn't know where to start learning about the intricacies of LinkedIn.

Jason Alba's I'm on LinkedIn—Now What??? *has opened up a whole new world to me and, as a result, to my clients as well. His honest, down-to-earth, and unpretentious style makes even the most complicated aspects of LinkedIn accessible and easy to understand, including concepts like the various degrees of contacts, which had me totally confused before. His simple, easy-to-follow, and sometimes ingenious instructions in every chapter have made it possible for me to make the best possible use of LinkedIn in my efforts to expand and market my business.*

I would strongly recommend this book to anyone who, like me, signed up for a LinkedIn membership with high hopes, then found themselves baffled as to how to proceed."

Lorraine Wright, Owner, 21st Century Resumes, http://www.21stcenturyresumes.ca

"Alba's book is the link you need to power up your LinkedIn results!"

Kent M. Blumberg, Executive and Professional Coach, Kent Blumberg Partners, http://www.KentBlumberg.com

"A few years ago, Jason Alba established his well-deserved place in the careers field as the go-to expert for LinkedIn. We look to him for advice on how to maximize LinkedIn for clients as well as seek his guidance about using LinkedIn to promote our businesses that cater to the millions of LinkedIn members. With each revision, he has added new and valuable tips. His latest edition is up-to-date, practical, and insightful. Jason rules LinkedIn!"

Debra Feldman, Executive Talent Agent, JobWhiz, http://www.jobwhiz.com

"I was ready to abandon my LinkedIn account before I read Jason Alba's concise and remarkably useful guide. Jason writes with remarkable clarity, provides one useful tip after another about how to use it most effectively, and unlike so many user guides that offer breathless and uncritical hype, Jason candidly explains the virtues and drawbacks of LinkedIn's features. Beyond that, Jason has such deep experience with the Web that the book contains hundreds of broader lessons about how to get the most of the Web. I learned an enormous amount from this little gem."

Robert Sutton, Professor, Stanford University; and Author, *The No Asshole Rule*, http://bobsutton.typepad.com/

"Jason offers a unique perspective on networking that's of interest to anyone that is a job seeker, entrepreneur, or networking enthusiast. He has been all of these, and his experiences with LinkedIn enable him to offer an integrated review for anyone to make the most of the LinkedIn tool. His book is a reflection of his deep understanding of people, technolog,y and change in the market, and can easily save the average new user months of time in trial and error."

Nadine Turner, Sarbanes-Oxley (SOX) IT Program Manager; and Six Sigma Black Belt

"If you are new to LinkedIn, you are in for a treat when you read I'm on LinkedIn— Now What??? *If this book were available the first year LinkedIn started, it would have helped LinkedIn to be better understood and would have helped thousands of professionals get the most out of LinkedIn."*

Vincent Wright, Chief Encouragement Officer, http://www.brandergy.com

"In an age of social networking, LinkedIn remains one of the best for business people. Jason gives a wonderful firsthand insight on the how-to's of using the service: this guide has been a long time coming. I am delighted that he's taken the time to put together, in a single volume, how to get the best out of the service."

Jack Yan, CEO, Jack Yan & Associates, http://www.jackyan.com

"Jason has written a great book for the beginner and those that need some more detailed instruction. This book is an easy read with some great descriptions of how to accomplish your LinkedIn networking tasks. I recommend this book for all users of LinkedIn."

Jim Browning, Co-owner/Lead Moderator, LinkedIn Atlanta; and President, Browning Business Solutions, LLC,
http://www.jimbrowningtraining.com

"Jason has written a highly practical guide to LinkedIn that will quickly allow a new user to understand and utilize LinkedIn. It's also a great guide to LinkedIn's hidden gems—finding high quality people through recommendations and from content found in Groups."
David Dalka, Senior Marketing and Business Development Professional, http://www.daviddalka.com

"This is a great book. I think Jason did an excellent job. I would recommend it to anyone who is just starting to build a LinkedIn network or for someone who has been a member for some time but is just now seeing the advantages LinkedIn provides."
Thom Allen, Writer and WordPress Consultant, http://www.thomallen.com

"I'm on LinkedIn—Now What??? provides a useful guide for all those looking to better utilize the power of LinkedIn. As Jason writes, LinkedIn is NOT the silver bullet of networking sites; such a site does not exist, and this book does not try to make that point. What this book does incredibly well is show how you CAN use the tool to your advantage—to make connections, to help others, and ultimately, to help yourself! Two handshakes WAY UP for this great book!"
Phil Gerbyshak, Author, *10 Ways to Make It Great!*; Owner, *The Make It Great Guy*, http://www.philgerbyshak.com/

"Jason's book is an easy-to-read, well-written, step-by-step tutorial for the novice, or for the person who's already linked in. He reveals his mastery, once again, at making the complex simple, just as he did with his invention of JibberJobber."
Billie R. Sucher, Career Transition Consultant; and Author, *Happy About the Career Alphabet*, http://www.billiesucher.com

"Jason Alba has established himself as a well- known and widely respected expert in the employment arena. His success in establishing himself and promoting his extraordinary career toolset JibberJobber.com prove that he knows what he's talking about. His understanding of personal branding and networking come together in his new book about using LinkedIn. Authoritative and insightful, this book is a great primer for 'newbies,' yet it's comprehensive enough to offer something of value to even the most seasoned LinkedIn users."
George Blomgren, Talent Acquisition Strategist

"You don't have to be a full-time social networker to use LinkedIn as a connection making tool and Jason Alba lays this out point by point in I'm on LinkedIn—Now What??? *in which he explains exactly how to use LinkedIn in a way that works for you. It's a book that I've long needed to explain just what LinkedIn is and isn't to countless friends and clients without buzzwords or hype; it's high on my list of recommendations."*
Susan Reynolds, New Media Consultant

*"As more and more business professionals hear about LinkedIn, they're looking for a place to go for answers about how to get involved and effectively use this important tool. Jason's book—*I'm on LinkedIn—Now What???* is appropriately titled and is the quickest and easiest way to understand what LinkedIn is, its purpose, and how to effectively use it. I'm an avid LinkedIn user, and regularly teach classes to busy professionals on how to use it for networking, job search, business development, or recruiting. One of the first things I do in all of my sessions is to recommend the book and the companion blog, because there are no other resources out there that cover how to get started and how to effectively use LinkedIn as well!"*

Jennifer McClure, Executive Recruiter/Executive Coach; and President, Unbridled Talent, LLC, http://unbridledtalent.com/blog

"Jason has a great knack for explaining the features and benefits of LinkedIn in a way that doesn't intimidate a novice. Yet he also includes little gems that can benefit even seasoned LinkedIn users. He clearly demonstrates how readers can benefit from LinkedIn in every chapter of I'm on LinkedIn—Now What??? *Readers will understand why they should do something rather than just being told that they should do it. This will bring more value to their LinkedIn experience."*

Christine Pilch, Co-owner of Grow My Company and Coauthor,
Understanding Brand Strategies: The Professional Service Firm's Guide to Growth, http://growmyco.com

"Jason's personal brand is consistent in each project he works on, especially in I'm on LinkedIn—Now What??? *Throughout this book he narrows down exactly what LinkedIn SHOULD be used for, so that readers don't confuse it with other social networks. You will encounter information on how to set up your profile, network through groups, and proper etiquette to use as you grow your LinkedIn database. Jason's thoughtful and honest viewpoint on LinkedIn will teach everyone from youthful professionals to experienced entrepreneurs how to succeed with this tool."*

Dan Schawbel, Managing Partner, Millennial Branding LLC; Author, *Me 2.0 and Promote Yourself*; and Publisher, Personal Branding Blog,
http://www.personalbrandingblog.com

CPSIA information can be obtained at www.ICGtesting.com
Printed in the USA
LVOW12s1641040614

388615LV00016B/741/P